Third G
Language

Language & Reading Workbook

Visit **McRuffy.com** for helpful resources to teach this curriculum!

Language & Reading Workbook (LAR)
ISBN 978159269-2088

McRuffy Press Third Grade Language Arts Curriculum
ISBN 978159269-2118

Written and illustrated by
Brian Davis M. A. Ed.

Graphic Design by
Sherylynn Davis

McRuffy Press, LLC
P.O. Box 212
Raymore, MO 64083

816-331-7831

sales@mcruffy.com

www.McRuffy.com

Go-Cart Games

Play games and race a go-cart on the back of the Language and Reading (LAR) workbook!

All games: In most games players answer a question or complete a task before earning a roll. Players will get a point for each correct answer or completed task. If a player lands on a space with a go-cart, players can complete a second task to roll again.

Players earn a point for each task completed successfully. Players also earn a point for being the first player to reach the FINISH space. Players may keep track of points using small objects such as counters, beans, or coins. Points can also be kept on paper as a scorecard. All players continue moving until they reach the FINISH space. The player with the most points wins.

Use a die, spinner, or draw numbers to move on the board with game pieces (small objects or game pawns).

Games (tasks to complete before moving) Play these games or make-up your own!

Vocabulary Word Game 1: A teacher or another player reads a definition. The player says the vocabulary word. You may also include words from previous weeks.

Vocabulary Word Game 2: A teacher or another player reads a vocabulary word. The player says a definition. Players do not have to say the definitions exactly how it was presented in the curriculum. They just have to give a good explanation of the meaning. You may also include words from previous weeks.

Vocabulary Word Game 3: A teacher or another player reads a vocabulary word. The player taking the turn uses it in a sentence correctly.

Parts of Speech Game: Use a Reading Book with the story from the current week. Roll and move first. Find a word for the part of speech that is indicated on the space. If you land on a go-cart space, find any word and tell its part of speech.

Find A Word Sentence Game: Use a Reading Book with the story from the current week. One player or teacher reads a sentence from a page in the story. Tell the player the page number of the sentence. The player taking the turn has to find the sentence and point it out in the book. You could use a timer and put a time limit on finding the sentence.

Answer Sentence Game: Use a Reading Book with the story from the current week. Find a sentence on this page that tells __________.

Finish the Sentence Game: Use a Reading Book with the story from the current week. One player or the teacher reads part of a sentence. The player taking the turn finishes the sentence. You may tell the player the page the sentence is on or a choice of two pages. You could use a timer and put a time limit on finding the sentence.

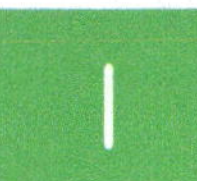

Read the clues. Find the word from the word list that answers the clue or completes the sentence. Write the answers in the boxes. Look at the arrows to decide if the words should be written down or across.

Across

1. Not clear
3. A cold place for food
5. This makes your voice loud.
6. This falls in a storm.
8. This is under your skin.
10. The color of the sky.
11. Birds are afraid of this.
13. To run away
14. Ice _______ cone
16. You can have this while sleeping.

Down

1. To remove clothes
2. It can explode.
4. Someone who makes things out of metal
7. A place to store things in a house.
8. Very short
9. This cleans teeth
12. To cook in a pan
14. You can see through things that are this.
15. Scared
17. You can see yours in a mirror.

flee fry toothbrush brief scarecrow blue blacksmith afraid
clear closet undress cream refrigerator blood firecracker
dream unclear raindrop microphone reflection

1

Read the words, definitions, and sample sentences.

consequences (con-se-quen-ces): *Things that happen because something else happened first.*

Joe did not put away his bike. A car drove over it.
Getting the bike smashed was a consequence for not putting it away.

comfortable (com-fort-a-ble): *Giving a cozy feeling or a relaxed feeling.*

The fluffy chair was very comfortable.

eavesdrop (eaves-drop): *Listening when the person speaking doesn't know you can hear them.*

Mother told Father about my birthday present. The didn't know I was eavesdropping.

expression (ex-pres-shun):

1. *A look on someone's face that tells how they are feeling.*

   I could tell by your expression that you have good news.

2. *A funny or different was to say something.*

   "Don't count your eggs before they hatch," is an expression.
   It means don't count on something until it happens.

favorite (fave-or-rit): *Something you like better than other things like it.*

Chocolate is my favorite flavor of ice cream.

handkerchief (hand-ker-chif): *A small square cloth used for wiping your mouth, eyes or nose.*

I wiped away the tears with the white handkerchief.

hopeless (hope-less): *Having no hope at all.*

Putting the shattered vase back together is hopeless.

minute (min-nut): *A measure of time, sixty seconds.*

We waited ten minutes for the bus.

tough (tuf): *Hard to tear, chew, break, or wear out.*

The steak was too tough to eat.

trough (trof): *Something that holds water. It's used by big animals for drinking.*

The cows drank the water from a trough.

Read the sentences. Some words are missing the second letter of blends. Write the sentences with the words corrected.

1. The bight fashlight binded the bullfog.

2. Mom deaded ceaning the refigerator.

3. A banket is in the coset.

4. Gandmother will dink the gass of grapefuit juice.

5. A fuzzy ceature is ceeping acoss the foor.

Poetry: Quatrain

A quatrain is a four line poem. Most follow a rhyming pattern.

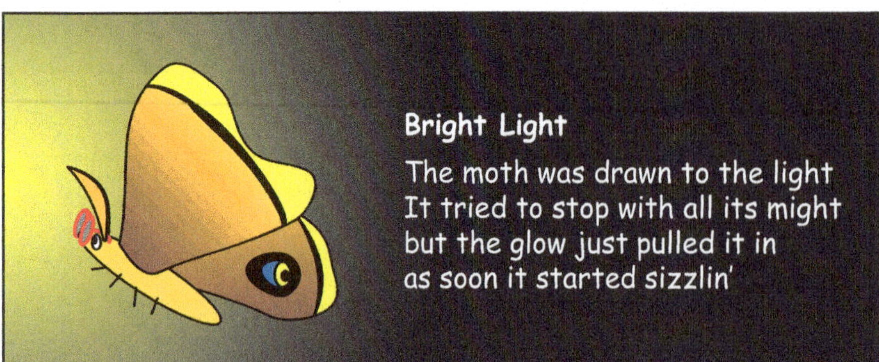

Bright Light

The moth was drawn to the light
It tried to stop with all its might
but the glow just pulled it in
as soon it started sizzlin'

Bright Light follows an AABB pattern. The first two lines rhyme and the last two lines rhyme.

Blueberry

Blueberry is my favorite pie
With filling round and blue
I'm sure if you will only try
You'll find you like it too

Blueberry follows an ABAB pattern. The first and third lines rhyme and the second and fourth lines rhyme.

Crayfish

The crayfish crawls in a creek
Fleeing flocks of floating ducks
Blended in, a small brown blob
With dreaded drakes drifting by

Crayfish does not have a rhyming pattern. It does feature **alliteration.** Crayfish, crawls, and creek all begin with the same sound. Using words that begin with the same sound is called alliteration. What other examples of alliteration are in the poem?

Answer the questions about the story.

A Tune for Tess

1. Addie was the name of
   - O A. the big red mule.
   - O B. the momma.
   - O C. the baby sister.

2. Old Tess was a
   - O A. fiddle.
   - O B. mule.
   - O C. fiddle and a mule.

3. What did Momma make with flour?
   - O A. blackberry pies
   - O B. bread
   - O C. cookies

4. Mr. Lucas was known as
   - O A. Mr. Fix-it.
   - O B. Mr. Mule-man.
   - O C. Mr. Fence-fixer.

5. The expression 'stretch a penny' means
   - O A. to spend wisely.
   - O B. to make the penny longer.
   - O C. to steal money.

6. Papa traded his first fiddle for
   - O A. the big red mule.
   - O B. the momma.
   - O C. the baby sister.

7. Each chapter had a title. Look in the book on page 3. The title of chapter 1 is The Big Red Mule. Read the titles for chapters 2 and 3. Chapter 4 does not have a title. What would be the best title for the chapter?
   - O A. to spend wisely.
   - O B. to make the penny longer.
   - O C. to steal money.

Poem Development: Refine your free writing. Look for possible rhymes and alliteration.

not
lot
bought
caught

red
bed
dread
fed
led
head
said
wed

dusty
dumpy
dark
dingy

I need to mow the lawn, but it's so hot outside. The mower is in the shed.
It's messy and dark in the shed. Sometimes the mower is hard to start.
If I were grass I don't think I would like to be mowed.

6

Read the words using the phonetic spellings and definitions.

awesome (aw-sum): *Something that deserves great respect*

café (ka-fay): *A place that cooks and serves food to people*

enough (ee-nuf): *The right amount*

explanation (eks-plan-a-shun): *Describing how something is done. or why something is the way it is.*

garage (ga-roj): *A shelter for a car*

miracle (mear-a-cul): *Something that God makes happen*

mountain (moun-tin): *A very high, rocky place*

obedient (o-bee-dee-ant): *Following the rules or directions*

quoted (quo-ted) *To repeat what someone has said or written*

Read the story the first time without filling in the blanks. Read it a second time. As you read, match the numbers to the vocabulary words that fill in the blanks.

Mountain Top Cafè

We ate lunch at the new __1__. It was at the top of a tall __2__. It was an __3__ sight. We took lots of photographs.

The road home was very steep. The traffic sign said to go slow. We tried to be __4__, but the brakes stopped working. The truck started moving too swiftly. It was out of control.

We prayed for a __5__. Suddenly, we saw a level side road. The truck coasted to a stop. We looked for an __6__ for the brake failure.

It had a broken part. We had the truck towed to a __7__. A man at the garage __8__ the price to get it fixed. We had __9__ money to get it fixed. Next time we'll eat in the valley instead of the mountain top.

_____ awesome   _____ café   _____ enough   _____ explanation   _____ garage

_____ miracle   _____ mountain   _____ obedient   _____ quoted

Read the sentences. Circle the nouns. Underline the verbs.

The river flowed swiftly over the rocks.

The obedient child followed her father.

Ann photographed the fireplace.

The skinny kitten drank the milk.

The snowflakes melted on the driveway.

Pick one of the sentences and change a noun. Write the new sentence.

Pick one of the sentences and change a verb. Write the new sentence.

8

Read the sentences. Fill in the circle that tells if the underlined noun is singular or plural.

1. The **boys** are swimming in the lake. ○ singular ○ plural
2. A **smudge** was on the photograph. ○ singular ○ plural
3. The **mountain** was awesome. ○ singular ○ plural
4. We ate at the new **cafè**. ○ singular ○ plural
5. Two **cars** were in the garage. ○ singular ○ plural

Pick a sentence with an underlined plural noun and make it singular.
Change other words to make it in agreement with the rest of the sentence.

Help Matt write a thank you letter to his grandparents for his birthday gift.

When you write a poem or a story, sometimes you can use a comparison that creates a word picture. There are two kinds of comparisons, **similes** and **metaphors**.

A **simile** compares two things using the words *like* or *as*.

Your smile is like a sunny day.

I can run as fast as a cheetah.

A **metaphor** compares too things and doesn't use *like* or *as*.

The clouds were puffy balls of cotton floating in the sky.

Write S or M in the boxes to identify the comparisons as similes or metaphors.

☐ The excited children were like a stampede of charging elephants.

☐ The apple was music to my taste buds.

☐ I was as frightened as a rabbit in a fox den.

Write a simile or a metaphor.

____

____

____

Poem Development: Refine your free writing. Look for possible rhymes and alliteration.

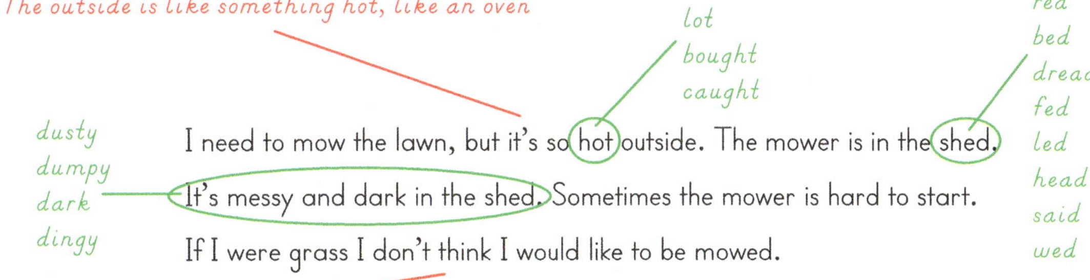

Answer the questions about the story, *The New Bike*.

Matthew wanted

- O A. a video game.
- O B. a bicycle.
- O C. Double Pump Slammers.

2. Rail's real name is

- O A. Robert.
- O B. Tommy.
- O C. Matthew.

3. The boys were making a

- O A. tree house.
- O B. fort.
- O C. go-cart.

4. Who gave Matthew money?

- O A. his parents
- O B. Rail's mother
- O C. his grandparents

5. Matthew hid money

- O A. in the tree house.
- O B. on his bicycle.
- O C. in a car.

6. Why was Matthew given money?

- O A. He earned it.
- O B. It was a present.
- O C. It was a reward.

7. What did Matthew do to his old bike?

____

____

____

8. Why did Rail's mother need money?

____

____

____

Read the story. Make a graph.

Toodles the monkey was going to have a party. It was going to be the best party ever. The party was for his good friend Gert the warthog. Toodles invited all of Gert's friends.

He knew how much they all liked to eat pies. Toodles asked all the animals he invited to tell him their favorite kind of pie.

Twelve monkeys liked banana pie the best. Seven warthogs loved chocolate pie. He asked five elephants to tell him their favorite pie. They all wanted peanut butter pie. The ten aardvarks all wanted ant pies. The nine alligators wanted monkey pie. Toodles said he would make them coconut pie instead. They said that would be fine.

With so much baking to do, Toodles decided he needed a graph. Make a graph for Toodles. Jungle animals eat a lot at parties. Each guest will get one pie. Show how many of each kind of pie Toodles will need.

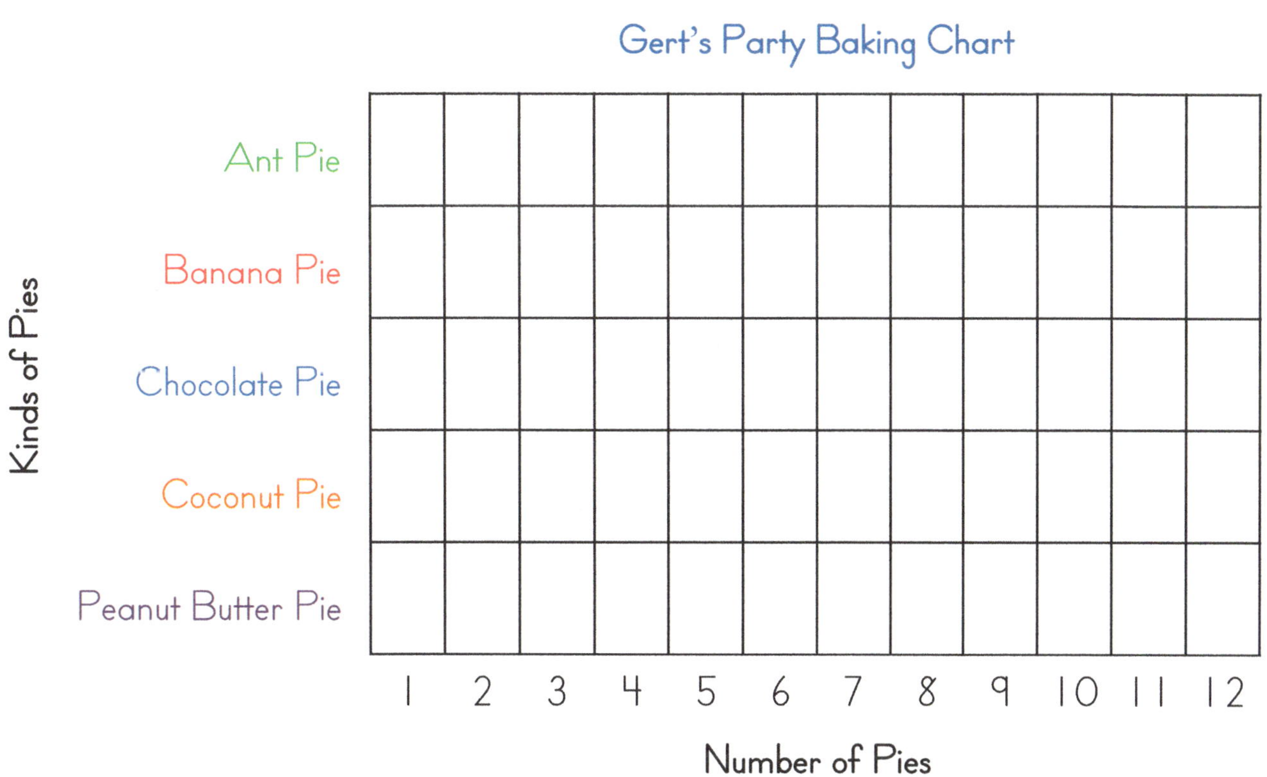

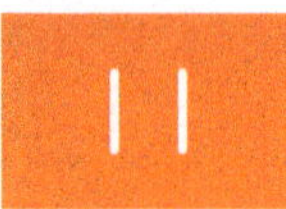

Read the words using the phonetic spellings and definitions.
Then write the number next to the sentence where it fits.

1. **envelope** (en-ve-lope): *a paper folder for mailing letters*
2. **embarrassed** (em-bare-essed): *to feel ashamed*
3. **disciplined** (dis-i-plind): *punishment or actions taken to learn something*

______ I was ____ when everyone stared at me.

______ The pup was ____ for chewing up the shoe.

______ The letter came in a brown ____ .

Read the sentences. A word is in bold print.
Fill in the circle next to the word that is a synonym to the word in bold print.

1. Can you **fix** the toaster?	O repair	O break	O clean
2. The horse **whinnied** at me.	O barked	O neighed	O smiled
3. The food is on the **platter**.	O fork	O tray	O oven
4. The **water** fell from the sky.	O bird	O leaves	O raindrops
5. The sharp knife will cut the **meat**.	O potatoes	O paper	O steak
6. Mother told me to **remain** here.	O leave	O stay	O look
7. That **bucket** weighs ten pounds.	O pail	O box	O pail
8. I don't like feeling **ashamed**.	O happy	O angry	O embarrassed
9. Matthew got a **gift** for his birthday.	O present	O cake	O spanking
10. We must stay on the **path** in the woods.	O sticks	O trail	O snakes

Read the sentences. Fill in the circle next to the pronoun that can take the place of the words in bold print.

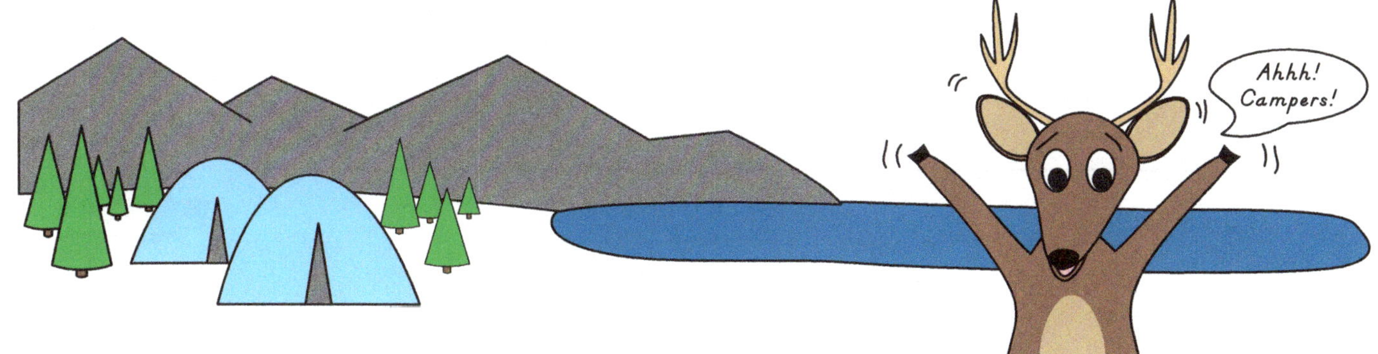

1. **The deer** was afraid of the campers. ○ He ○ She ○ They ○ It
2. **Sue** bought a new raincoat. ○ He ○ She ○ They ○ It
3. **The cats** hissed at the dog. ○ He ○ She ○ They ○ It
4. **The boy** saw a reindeer. ○ He ○ She ○ They ○ It
5. Did the rock break **the window**? ○ He ○ She ○ They ○ It
6. **My father** carried the pail. ○ He ○ She ○ They ○ It
7. **The girl** mailed the letters. ○ He ○ She ○ They ○ It
8. **The boxes** weighed twelve pounds. ○ He ○ She ○ They ○ It
9. **A man** paid for the grain. ○ He ○ She ○ They ○ It
10. **That snail** is very slow. ○ He ○ She ○ They ○ It

Poem Development: Get rid of extra words. Add any similes, metaphors, rhymes, or alliteration to complete your poem.

The yard was like a blazing oven
I dug into the dark and dusty shed
I pulled the rope and started shovin'
A roaring monster filling grass with dread

13

Read the sentences. Answer the questions about the pronouns.

Example: Stan carried the vase. He tripped and dropped it.

Who is he? *Stan* What is it? *vase*

1. The cars honked at the puppy. It barked at them.

   What it them? ______________ What is it? ______________

2. My uncle saw my mother. He gave her a hug.

   Who is her? ______________ Who is he? ______________

3. Sally is nice to her brother. She gave him an ice cream cone.

   Who is him? ______________ Who is she? ______________

4. The crowd loved the funny monkey. They laughed at the tricks it did.

   Who are they? ______________ What is it? ______________

5. The mouse saw the snake. It bit it.

   ____

Write a homophone for each word by spelling the long a sound a different way.

Example: ate *eight*

1. break ______________
2. weigh ______________
3. reign ______________
4. mail ______________
5. wait ______________
6. tale ______________
7. prey ______________
8. grate ______________

Writing a Research Report

1. Choose a topic
2. Think of possible questions you or your reader might want answered. You may want to make a graphic organizer of your questions.

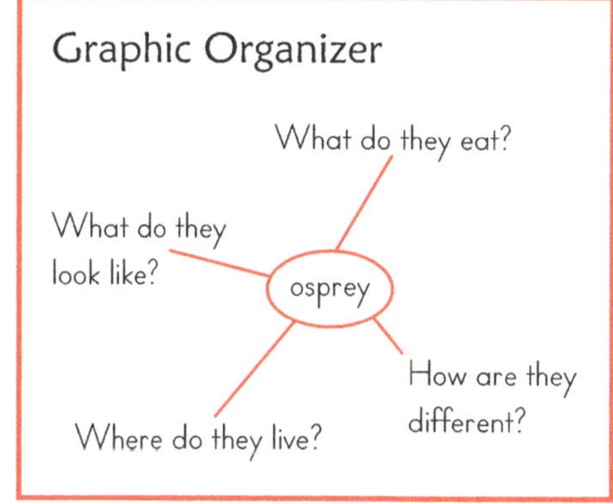

3. Find information: websites, magazines, topical books, reference books such as encyclopedias and dictionaries, and experts. Be sure to keep track of your sources and give them credit.

   If you copy a source word for word, be sure to use quotation marks. This indicates that you are not trying to make others think these are your own words.

   Make notes of your information. Note cards are helpful because you can rearrange them to help organize your report.

4. Organize your report. Make an outline or create another graphic organizer.

Write a report about osprey. Use the outline below and any additional information you may find from your own research. Change the outline if you would like or create your own.

Osprey

I. Other Names
   A. Fishhawk
   B. Seahawk
   C. Fishing Eagle

II. Food
   A. Fish

III. Size
   A. 24" long
   B. Six foot wingspan

IV. Color
   A. White head and underparts
   B. Brown around eyes, wings, and back

V. Habitat
   A. Worldwide except Antarctica
   B. Lives near water

VI. Unusual Characteristics
   A. Reversible toe and rounded talons help catch fish
   B. Can see fish while flying over 100 feet above water
   C. Likes to build nests on man-made objects

15

Answer the questions about the story, *Happy Birthday*.

1. The puppy's name is
   - O A. Buster.
   - O B. Buddy.
   - O C. Sweet Pea.

2. Matthew turned ____ years old.
   - O A. eight
   - O B. nine
   - O C. ten

3. The pup chewed Matthew's
   - O A. homework.
   - O B. hat.
   - O C. boots.

4. The pup chased a
   - O A. car.
   - O B. truck.
   - O C. car and a truck.

5. Matthew tied the pup to
   - O A. a rock.
   - O B. a tree.
   - O C. a trash can.

6. Mr. Day was going to build a
   - O A. fence.
   - O B. doghouse.
   - O C. tree house.

7. Why did Rachel get grounded?

____

____

____

8. What did Matthew learn about discipline?

____

____

____

Read the story.

Dark clouds rolled over the forest. Soon, large raindrops began to fall. The animals ran for shelter. The army of ants scrambled for their hole in the ground. That is, all except one. Elma that ant was tugging a strange object. She had found it at a campsite. It had the letters t-o-o-t-h-p-a-s-t-e printed on it.

"Plug the hole!" yelled the commander of the ant troop. His name was Bizmo. "The water must remain outside."

"But Elma is not here. We can't leave her outside," said another ant.

Water was already beginning to fill the hole. Bizmo surveyed the rushing water. "We must think of what is best for all," said Bizmo. "We have to stop the water. The whole ant nation is at risk."

The ants tried to plug the hole. The weight of the water was too great. Elma tugged and tugged when she saw what was happening. Suddenly a great gush of water picked up the tube of toothpaste. Elma hopped on.

It floated right to the ant's hole. Elma jumped into the hole. Then a tree limb crashed down. It landed on the tube. Toothpaste squirted into the hole. The water stopped running in Elma's toothpaste had stopped the water. The ants were saved.

The next day was clear and sunny. The ants had a celebration for Elma. They wanted to repay her for being so brave. Then they had a great feast. The ants thought the toothpaste tasted very yummy.

Number the sets of sentences in the order they happened in the story from 1 to 3.

Set 1

____ Bizmo ordered the ants to plug the hole.
____ Raindrops began to fall.
____ An ant said that Elma was missing.

Set 2

____ A gush of water picked up the toothpaste.
____ Elma hopped onto the tube of toothpaste.
____ Water rushed into the ant's hole.

Set 3

____ Toothpaste squirted in the hole.
____ A limb fell on the tube.
____ Elma jumped into the hole.

Set 4

____ The water stopped coming in.
____ The ants had a celebration.
____ The next day was sunny.

What would be a good title for this story?

____

16

Vocabulary: Read the words and definitions.

artificial (ar-ti-fi-shul): *Something that is made to be like something else.*

customer (cus-tum-er): *A person who buys things.*

explosion (ek-splo-shun): *A sudden release of power.*

identification (i-den-ti-fi-kay-shun): *Something that tells other people who you are.*

invention (in-ven-shun): *Something new that someone discovers or makes.*

laboratory (lab-ru-tor-ee): *A room used for learning scientific things.*

millionaire (mill-yu-nair): *A person who owns things worth a million dollars or more.*

occasionally (u-kay-shun-ul-ee): *Something that happens only now and then.*

ordinary (or-di-nair-ee): *Something that is common or not unusual.*

Write the vocabulary word that completes each sentence.

The scientist worked in the ______________________.

A ______________________ owns the huge house.

The light bulb was a great ______________________.

The animal scratching at the door was not an ______________________ cat.

The policeman showed us his badge for ______________________.

The ______________________ waited to pay for her food.

Leaking gas can cause an ______________________.

It ______________________ snows in November.

The ______________________ fruit is made of wax.

Read the sentences. Fill in the circle next to the word that is an adjective.

1. Five mice played on the pipe.	○ Five	○ mice	○ pipe
2. Did Dad buy the new bike?	○ Did	○ new	○ bike
3. The quiet child seemed quite sad.	○ quiet	○ child	○ sad
4. The blue kite was caught on a line.	○ blue	○ kite	○ caught
5. Who ate the hot French fries?	○ Who	○ ate	○ hot
6. A fly landed by the apple pie.	○ fly	○ landed	○ apple
7. We might see a rare eagle in the sky.	○ might	○ rare	○ sky
8. The child had a mild fever.	○ had	○ mild	○ fever
9. A nice boy was sitting behind me.	○ nice	○ behind	○ me
10. The red sign said to stay out.	○ sign	○ red	○ stay

18

Read the sentences. Underline the verb.
Does the verb have the past or present tense?
Fill in the circle.

1. The bear is driving the car. ○ past ○ present
2. The bird is flying to its nest. ○ past ○ present
3. I liked the chocolate cake. ○ past ○ present
4. We stopped when we saw the deer. ○ past ○ present
5. The nine ducks walked to the pond. ○ past ○ present

Change the tense of the sentences and rewrite them.

The scientist is making a new invention.

____

____

The customer bought the artificial flowers.

____

____

Think of an invention. Answer the questions to write about it.

Inventor's name ________________________________

What is it called? ________________________________

How does it work? ________________________________

____

____

____

What is it made of? ________________________________

How will it help people or why would people want it? ________________

____

____

____

Draw a picture of your invention.

20

Answer the questions about the story, *The Wrong Goal*.

1. The headband
   - O A. beeped
   - O B. rang
   - O C. buzzed

2. Megan was
   - O A. farsighted
   - O B. too slow
   - O C. nearsighted

3. Megan kicked the ball at
   - O A. a popcorn stand.
   - O B. a bird's nest.
   - O C. both A and B

4. What was Onyx?
   - O A. Megan's coach
   - O B. a computer
   - O C. both A and B

5. Allison's dog was named
   - O A. Buster.
   - O B. Fluffy.
   - O C. Ruff.

6. Megan got new
   - O A. chipmunks.
   - O B. glasses.
   - O C. soccer shoes.

7. What caught on fire?
   - O A. a building
   - O B. a fire truck
   - O C. grass

8. How old was Allison?
   - O A. eight
   - O B. nine
   - O C. ten

9. How did Megan play in the next soccer game?

____

____

____

10. What did Allison learn in the story?

____

____

____

Read and follow the directions:

Winston needed to take the FRV–7 for some test flights. Allison made a map of the farm. It was her job to give her father directions. After each flight, the FRV–7 flew back to the launch pad and started over.

Read the directions and write where the FRV-7 went on each test flight.

Test Flight 1: Go over three spaces and down two spaces. ____________________

Test Flight 2: Go down two spaces and over one space. ____________________

Test Flight 3: Go over five spaces. ____________________

Test Flight 4: Go over four spaces and down three spaces. ____________________

Test Flight 5: Go down two spaces. Go over five spaces. Go up one space. ____________________

____

Test Flight 6: Go over four spaces and down one space. ____________________

Test Flight 7: Go down three spaces. ____________________

Test Flight 8: Go down three spaces and over two spaces then up two spaces. ____________________

____

FRV–7 Launch Pad			Pig Pen		Bird's Nest
		Barn		Flock of Geese	Pond
	Flower Garden		Field		
Laboratory		Chickens		House	

21

Read the words and the definitions.

companies (cum-pa-nees): *Businesses*

cousin (cus-in): *The child of your aunt or uncle*

curiosity (cur-ee-os-i-tee): *A feeling of wanting to know more about something*

different (diff-e-rent or dif-rent): *Unlike in some way*

disappointed (dis-e-poin-tid): *Feeling unhappy because hopes were not met*

electricity (ee-lec-tris-e-tee): *The power that flows through wires*

machine (mu-sheen): *Something that does work or makes things*

Read the story. Match the blanks to vocabulary words. Write the numbers next to the words at the bottom of the page.

My __1__ Karen said she was taking me to a show. I expected to see a movie or play. Then she told me it was a __2__ kind of show.

When businesses want people to see the things they make, they have shows. Lots of __3__ had their products on the display.

There were many unusual inventions. One __4__ created lots of __5__. I had never seen anything like it. It looked like it was holding two pizzas.

A lady told me that the discs were covered with solar cells. The solar cells let the machine make __6__ from sunlight. The machine was being made to explore the planet Mars. I really enjoyed the show. Although it wasn't a movie, I wasn't __7__.

_____ companies _____ cousin _____ curiosity _____ different

_____ disappointed _____ electricity _____ machine

Write a word that means more than one of each word. (Write the plural form.)

Example: man men

1. wolf ______
2. tooth ______
3. mouse ______
4. shelf ______
5. goose ______
6. deer ______
7. woman ______
8. child ______
9. knife ______
10. calf ______

Choose the singular or plural form to complete the sentences.

The ______ are in the field.

The ______ is on the lake.

The ______ chewed on the doughnut.

The ______ are in the cage.

23

Read the sentences. Write a Q in the box if the sentence is a question. Write an S if the sentence is a statement. Put the correct ending marks at the end of the sentences, periods, or question marks.

☐ 1. Do Inuit people make igloos____

☐ 2. The electricity went off at the hotel____

☐ 3. My poem was very different____

☐ 4. Where is the old automobile____

☐ 5. Did the sink overflow____

☐ 6. How did my raincoat get ripped____

☐ 7. My cousin loves avocados____

☐ 8. Who unplugged the toaster____

☐ 9. The wheelbarrow lost a wheel____

☐ 10. Why do doughnut have holes____

Write a statement and a question.

Statement:

____

____

____

Question:

____

____

____

Writing a Good Paragraph

A paragraph has three parts. it begins with a **topic sentence**. It has **supporting sentences** that add details. It ends with a **closing sentence** that sums up the paragraph's main idea. Include all three parts for a well-constructed paragraph.

A funny thing happened Angie burnt a doughnut.

Detail 1 Angie watched Mom put a bagel in the toaster.

Detail 2 Angie wanted a warm doughnut.

Detail 3 The toaster started smoking.

Indent the first word in a paragraph. →

My little sister, Angie, learns the funniest things from watching others. One day she got a doughnut stuck in the toaster. She had watched Mom heat us a bagel. Angie thought it was a doughnut. She wanted a warm doughnut, too, When the toaster started smoking, Angie thought it was going to explode. She ran screaming to my mother. Mom didn't think it was too funny when she saw the mess, but I couldn't stop laughing.

Make notes to write a paragraph about a funny event.

A funny thing happened ____________________

Detail 1 ____________________

Detail 2 ____________________

Detail 3 ____________________

25

Answer the questions about the story, *One is Enough*.

1. Who acted like a dog?

   ○ A. Emily
   ○ B. Elaine
   ○ C. Allison

2. What was stolen?

   ○ A. FRV-7
   ○ B. Onyx
   ○ C. People Copy Machine

3. What did Elaine hear in an office?

   ○ A. a mouse
   ○ B. Fluffy
   ○ C. Uncle Winston

4. What is Allison's mom's name?

   ○ A. Anna
   ○ B. Barbara
   ○ C. Cathy

5. Why did Allison build the People Copy Machine?

   ○ A. She wanted to help her dad.
   ○ B. She wanted to make a copy of Emily.
   ○ C. She needed a science fair project.

Read the paragraph. Answer the questions.

The word automobile comes from two words. *Auto* means self. *Mobile* means able to be moved. So *automobile* means to move by itself. The first automobiles looked like wagons. The looked strange to people used to seeing horses pull wagons. It's no wonder people called the automobiles.

1. What did the early automobiles look like? ______________________
2. What does the word *auto* mean? ______________________
3. What does the word *mobile* mean? ______________________

Read the letter. The words are wrong. The words in color print are the homophones for the correct words. Write the correct words on the lines under the letter.

Deer Sally,

I've been meaning to **right** you for **sum** time. I can't **weight** to **sea** you again. You don't **no** how I've missed **ewe**. **Wood** you visit me soon?

Eye maid a cake this **mourning**. It didn't cost much. The **flower** was on **sail**. I **eight** most of it. It tasted **grate**. I'll bake you **won** when you come.

Your Friend,

Buzz

_______________ _______________ _______________

_______________ _______________ _______________

_______________ _______________ _______________

_______________ _______________ _______________

_______________ _______________ _______________

____

Vocabulary words for *One is Enough* part 2.

attention (a-ten-shun): *To listen or watch closely*

recognize (re-cog-nize): *To know what something is or know who someone is*

underneath (un-der-neeth): *Below something*

warehouse (ware-hous): *A large building used to store things*

The _______________ was full of boxes.

I did not _______________ you in that costume.

You should pay _______________ to your parents.

There is a badger _______________ the porch.

What part of speech matches the color of the words? Fill in the circles to mark your answer.

They quietly watched a cartoon about a blue kangaroo.

O noun	O pronoun	O verb	O adverb	O adjective
O noun	O pronoun	O verb	O adverb	O adjective
O noun	O pronoun	O verb	O adverb	O adjective
O noun	O pronoun	O verb	O adverb	O adjective
O noun	O pronoun	O verb	O adverb	O adjective

The old bloodhound howled loudly at her poodle

O noun	O pronoun	O verb	O adverb	O adjective
O noun	O pronoun	O verb	O adverb	O adjective
O noun	O pronoun	O verb	O adverb	O adjective
O noun	O pronoun	O verb	O adverb	O adjective
O noun	O pronoun	O verb	O adverb	O adjective

Read the sentences. Circle the helping verbs. Underline the verb it helps.

1. The mongoose was chasing the snake.
2. The poodles were barking at the cats.
3. The slippers are falling off the footstool.
4. A cartoon is playing on the television.
5. I am working at the warehouse.
6. The woodpecker was hunting for bugs.
7. The children were leaving the school.
8. The kangaroo is hopping across the yard.
9. I am paying attention to my mother.
10. The bloodhounds are howling in the moonlight.

Unscramble the sentences. Write them on the lines.

was the the leaves moose chewing

oven cookies the baked in we the

Combine the sentences. Use the word *and*.

Woodpeckers have long tongues. Their tongues are sticky.

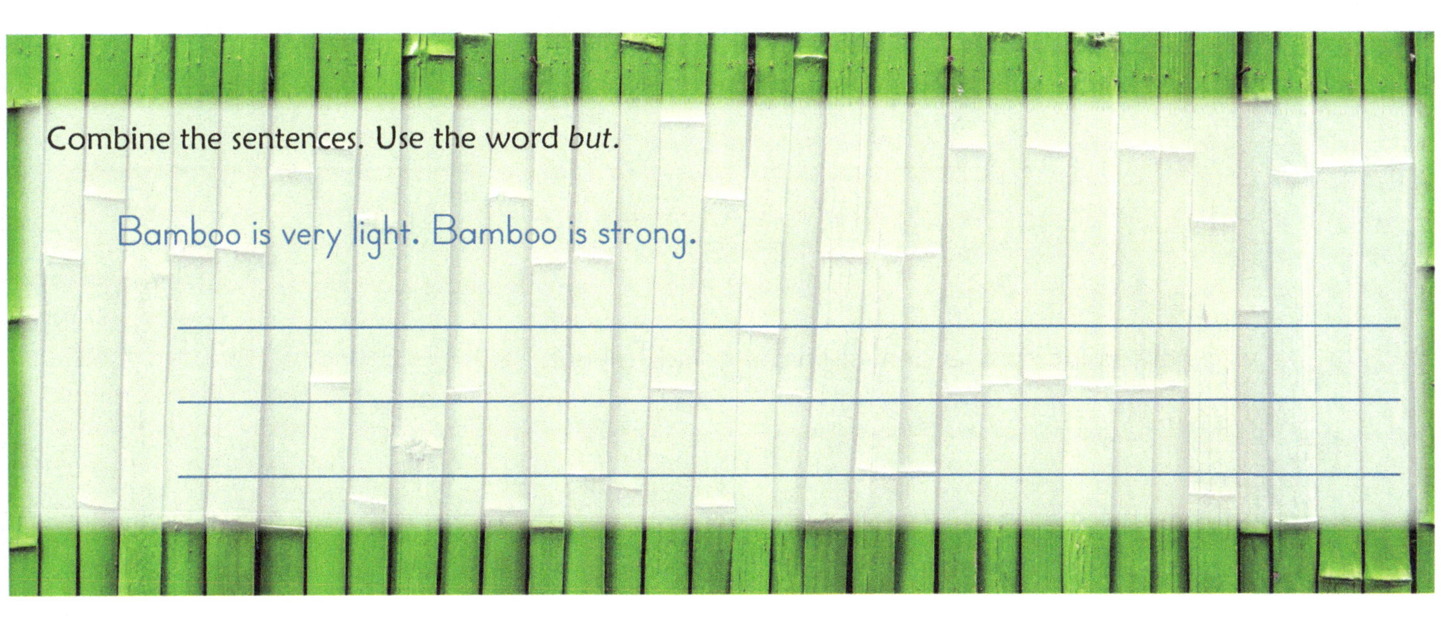

Combine the sentences. Use the word *but*.

Bamboo is very light. Bamboo is strong.

Read the sentences. Make inferences to answer the questions.

1. Kevin hit the baseball. The window shattered.
   How did the window get broken?

2. The thunder shook the house. Water dripped from the ceiling.
   Why was water dripping from the ceiling?

3. We forgot about the cookies. Smoke poured from the oven.
   What happened to the cookies?

4. The sugar jar tipped over. Mom handed me a broom.
   What happened to the sugar?

5. It was getting loose. The dentist said it could fall out.
   What was getting loose?

Answer the questions about the story, *One is Enough*.

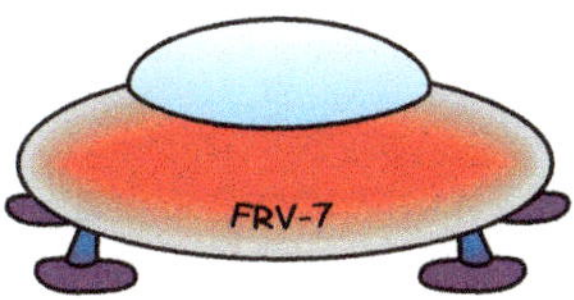

1. What does the FRV in FRV-7 stand for?

2. The man that was kidnapped was the president of what?

3. Elaine and Onyx solved a problem that Winston had with the FRV-7. What was the problem?

4. What did the police think when they first saw the FRV-7?

5. Why do you think the story was called One is Enough?

Write a long e word to match each description.

1. Something I call myself ______________________
2. It swings on trees and eats bananas. ______________________
3. Someone who steals things ______________________
4. Smile to show this mood ______________________
5. A sandy place by the sea ______________________
6. A place to put socks ______________________

Read the sentences. What word is an antonym to the word in bold print?
Fill in the circle next to the correct answer.

1. The water was very **shallow.** ○ cold ○ low ○ deep
2. **She** pulled the weeds. ○ Sally ○ He ○ Bees
3. The puppy was very **nice.** ○ mean ○ kind ○ fluffy
4. The meeting was very **long.** ○ boring ○ brief ○ peaceful
5. The king was a **jolly** fellow. ○ nutty ○ silly ○ grumpy
6. The peaches were **dirty.** ○ sweet ○ clean ○ muddy
7. The story made us **laugh.** ○ weep ○ giggle ○ sing
8. The money was **fake.** ○ green ○ real ○ mine

Add letters to the words to make the lone e sound.
Rewrite the words on the lines.

Example: lash leash

1. fort ______ 2. chef ______

3. best ______ 4. wed ______

5. sill ______ 6. fast ______

7. met ______ 8. turk ______

Read the sentences. Fill in the circle next to the word that is an adverb.

1. The deer quickly crossed the road. O deer O quickly O crossed

2. The queen spoke softly. O queen O spoke O softly

3. The chief briefly used the shield. O chief O briefly O shield

4. Pete deeply loved his sheep. O deeply O loved O sheep

5. The children slowly fell asleep. O slowly O feel O asleep

6. The food was needed badly. O food O needed O badly

7. The bunny swiftly hopped along the path. O bunny O swiftly O hopped

8. The sleepy baby cried loudly. O sleepy O baby O loudly

9. The lion roared fiercely. O lion O roared O fiercely

10. Cheaply made toys break easily. O cheaply O made O break

33

Read the sentences. Add an adverb and rewrite the sentences.

Example: The boy raised his hand. *The boy meekly raised his hand.*

1. The sheep ran from the wolf.

2. Steve swatted at the bee.

3. The farmer plowed the field.

4. The knight picked up a shiny shield.

Write a letter in each blank to match the cause to the effect.

The ice fell all night long. The roads became very slick. A dog crossed the road. A car tried to stop. The car spun and hit a truck. The truck ran off the road. It hit a pole. The pole cracked. The cracking sound woke me up.

The pole broke. The power lines fell. Our house was dark. I got out of bed. My brother left a roller skate on the floor. I couldn't see it. I tripped and fell. I landed on my new painting. It turned my blue pajamas red and green. I had to wash my pajamas in the sink. It made the sink a mess. It was a very long night.

1. _____ The ice fell all night long.	A. I couldn't see the skate.
2. _____ The pole broke.	B. The sink was a mess.
3. _____ My painting wasn't dry.	C. The roads became slick.
4. _____ A dog crossed the road.	D. A car tried to stop.
5. _____ Our house was dark.	E. The power lines fell.
6. _____ A car hit a truck.	F. I tripped and fell.
7. _____ There was a loud cracking sound.	G. Red and green paint got on me.
8. _____ I washed my pajamas.	H. I woke up.
9. _____ My brother left a skate on the floor.	I. The truck ran off the road.

Make up your own cause and effect sentences.

____

____

____

____

35

Answer the questions about the story, *Like Layers of an Onion*.

1. Buster dug a hole
   - O A. under the fence.
   - O B. in a garden
   - O C. both A and B

2. Buster chased a
   - O A. squirrel
   - O B. cat
   - O C. both A and B

3. What happened to the shovel?
   - O A. It broke.
   - O B. Matthew lost it.
   - O C. Busters chewed it.

4. What had glue on it?
   - O A. Matthew
   - O B. a bird
   - O C. a squirrel

5. The bulldog was covered with
   - O A. glue.
   - O B. onions.
   - O C. paint.

6. What did Matthew have to buy?
   - O A. a garbage can
   - O B. a rope
   - O C. a birdhouse

7. Who owned a garden?
   - O A. Mr. Day
   - O B. The Andersons
   - O C. Mr. Johnson

8. Matthew broke
   - O A. a ladder.
   - O B. a window.
   - O C. a hammer.

9. How are lies like onions?

____

____

____

____

Read the questions. Answer them using the review vocabulary words.

1. This is a place to eat. ____________________
2. This is something you get in the mail. ____________________
3. This is a place where a scientist works. ____________________
4. This means it is not really what it seems like. ____________________
5. This is the child of your uncle. ____________________
6. These are bad ways to feel. ______________ and ______________
7. This means to listen when you're not supposed to. ____________________

Read the sentences. Find a word that matches each part of speech.

1. He was carefully carrying the injured poodle.

noun ____________ pronoun ____________ adjective ____________

verb ____________ adverb ____________ helping verb ____________

2. They were tugging fiercely on the slippery nets.

noun ____________ pronoun ____________ adjective ____________

verb ____________ adverb ____________ helping verb ____________

3. The red automobile is honking loudly at us.

noun ____________ pronoun ____________ adjective ____________

verb ____________ adverb ____________ helping verb ____________

37

Read the sentences. Underline the verb. Does the verb have the past or present tense? Fill in the circle.

1. The moose chewed its food. ○ past ○ present
2. A raccoon hides behind the boot. ○ past ○ present
3. We take the books to this room. ○ past ○ present
4. The boat tipped over in the flood. ○ past ○ present
5. A balloon floats above the roof. ○ past ○ present

Read the paragraphs. Answer the questions.

A mongoose is a small furry animal. It is about 16 to 24 inches long. Its shaggy fur is brown or gray. It digs holes in the ground. This helps it catch its food. A mongoose will eat snakes, birds, mice, and other animals.

1. What color of fur does a mongoose have?

   ○ black or white ○ brown or gray ○ purple and green

2. What does a mongoose eat?

   ○ seeds and grass ○ burgers and fries ○ snakes and birds

3. How big is a mongoose?

   ○ 16 to 24 pounds ○ 16 to 24 inches ○ 16 to 24 feet

Mindy went to the zoo on Tuesday. She saw monkeys swinging from trees. Bears splashed in a pool of water. Her favorite animals were the kangaroos. One of them had a joey in its pouch. A joey is a baby kangaroo. Most of all, Mindy liked to watch them hop. Their powerful legs helped them hop over twenty feet at a time.

4. What played in a pool of water?

   ○ bears ○ monkeys ○ kangaroos

5. What is a baby kangaroo called?

   ○ Mindy ○ babyroo ○ Joey

6. What day did Mindy visit the zoo?

   ○ Tuesday ○ Saturday ○ Wednesday

Read the pairs of words. Are they synonyms or antonyms? Fill in the correct circles.

1. **embarrassed**, proud O synonym O antonym
2. **suddenly**, slowly O synonym O antonym
3. **drenched**, soaked O synonym O antonym
4. **frighten**, scare O synonym O antonym
5. **cool**, warm O synonym O antonym

Read the sentences. A helping verb is needed.
Rewrite the sentences with the correct helping verb for each tense.

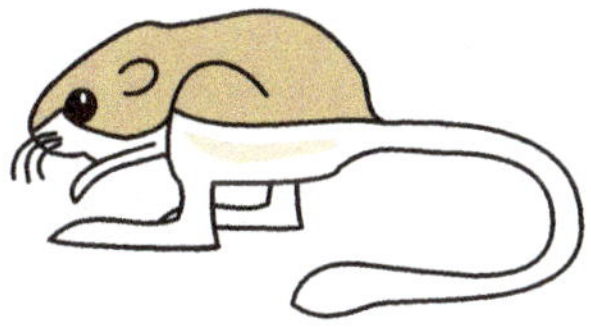

1. The kangaroo rat hopping.

past tense: ______________________________

____

present tense: ______________________________

____

2. The doughnuts cooling off.

past tense: ______________________________

____

present tense: ______________________________

____

3. I writing a story.

past tense: ______________________________

____

present tense: ______________________________

____

Read the words and definitions.

advertisement: *something used to draw attention to a product or an event*

allowance: *money given to a child by a parent*

autograph: *to write one's name on something*

contestant: *someone who tries to win a prize*

decision: *making up one's mind*

distracted: *to think about one thing while doing another thing*

idol: *someone or something that is worshiped that shouldn't be worshiped*

imaginary: *not real, pretend*

jealous: *afraid of losing love or attention*

nervous: *uneasy or fearful*

secretary: *someone who helps work in an office*

Write vocabulary words to answer the questions or complete the sentences.

What words are feelings? ____________________ ____________________

If I'm in a race, I'm a ____________________

What is something you'll see in newspapers? ____________________

If your parents give you money every week, what is that called? ____________________

If you're not paying attention, what are you? ____________________

What is it called when someone famous writes their name for you? ____________________

If you call an office, who might answer the phone? ____________________

If I said a six-foot tall invisible rabbit was standing next to you, what kind of rabbit would it be? ____________________

Read the description. Make a new word to match it by choosing a word from list A and adding a word from list B to the end of it.

Example: rabbit food carrot

List A	List B
wag	den
car	set
hid	on
cab	sect
sun	rot
in	in

1. It happens at night. ______________________
2. It's a small house. ______________________
3. It's another name for a bug. ______________________
4. It's something not easy to see. ______________________
5. It has four wheels and hauls things. ______________________

Read the sentences. Circle the prepositions. Choose a different proposition from the word list in the orange box and write the sentence with a new preposition. Choose a different preposition for each sentence.

past between behind above near among

1. The dog is on the bike.

____

2. The horse ran to the trees.

____

3. We sat underneath the waterfall.

____

43

Read the story about Rosa. She is an eight-year-old girl who lives in a country in Central America. Then, read the sentences at the bottom of the page.

My name is Rosa. I live in a country called Costa Rica. In Spanish it means "Rich Coast". My country is south of the United States. It is a small country, but it is a great country. About two and a half million people live here. That is less than many cities in the United States.

My home is on a farm. A farm is the best place to live. We grow rice, corn, and beans to eat. I also have a few chickens. They are fun pets to have. They lay eggs that taste good.

We grow something else on the farm. Papa grows coffee beans. The dark red beans grow on bushes. Picking coffee beans is hard work. That is why I like to help my papa. We also have two banana trees. Bananas are the best tasting fruits.

There are mountains in Costa Rica. Some of the mountains are volcanoes. The smoke from them smells bad. An ocean is on one side of our country. A sea is on the other side. If you like water, you'll like Costa Rica.

1. Costa Rica is a country. ○ fact ○ opinion
2. Costa Rica is south of the United States. ○ fact ○ opinion
3. Bananas are the best tasting fruits. ○ fact ○ opinion
4. Smoke from volcanoes smells bad. ○ fact ○ opinion
5. Coffee beans grow in Costa Rica. ○ fact ○ opinion
6. A farm is the best place to live. ○ fact ○ opinion
7. Coffee beans grow on bushes. ○ fact ○ opinion
8. Rosa's farm has two banana trees. ○ fact ○ opinion
9. Picking coffee beans is hard word. ○ fact ○ opinion
10. Chickens are fun pets. ○ fact ○ opinion

Read the words. Write a sentence telling how they are alike.
Use a spelling word in the sentence.

wagon lemon object spinach music astonish
rather adventure giant rectangle insect
amusement hungry cactus number

1. banjo, harmonic, piano

____

____

2. wasp, ant, ladybug

____

____

3. juice, peel, pulp

____

____

4. fifty, seven, sixteen

____

____

5. roller coaster, merry-go-round, bumper cars

____

____

45

Read the questions about the story, *The Sky's the Limit*. Answer them with complete sentences.

1. Who did Matthew want to meet?

2. What did Matthew learn in the story?

3. What idea did Sky Bordon get from Matthew?

Read the paragraphs. Fill in the circle next to the sentence that states the main idea.

1. Mom bought six big bags of apples. She will bake tasty pies with the apples. Then, she will fill jars with brown apple butter. For supper she will fix baked apples. I'm getting hungry already.

   Choose the main idea:

   - O A. I'm getting hungry
   - O B. Mom bakes great apple pies.
   - O C. Mom makes lots of things with apples.
   - O D. Mom bought six big bags of apples.

2. We heard a honking sound in the driveway. It didn't sound like a car horn. "Who is here?" asked my sister. I looked outside. There wasn't a car or truck in the driveway. I was astonished to see what was honking. It was a whole flock of geese.

   Choose the main idea:

   - O A. My sister was astonished.
   - O B. Geese were in the driveway.
   - O C. A car was honking at a truck.
   - O D. I looked out into the driveway.

Read the descriptions.
Write a long oo word to fill in the blanks.

canoe	coupon	screwdriver	
barbecue	jewelry	pursue	cougar

1. This cat could scare dogs. ______________________
2. This is a way to cook food outside. ______________________
3. Use this at a store to save money. ______________________
4. This means to chase or seek something. ______________________
5. You can travel on a stream in this. ______________________
6. This is a handy tool. ______________________
7. It's made of gold and diamonds. ______________________

Read the words and definitions.

determined: *make a final decision*

immediately: *right away, instantly*

important: *very necessary or meaningful*

impossible: *not able to be done*

ordinarily: *what usually happens*

responsible: *expected to take care of duties*

stopwatch: *a special watch used for timing events to less than a second*

Read the sentences. Find and circle the words that have the long oo sound.

1. My new shoes are covered with blue goo.
2. Is Bruce through eating the soup?
3. You should choose to chew beefy stew.

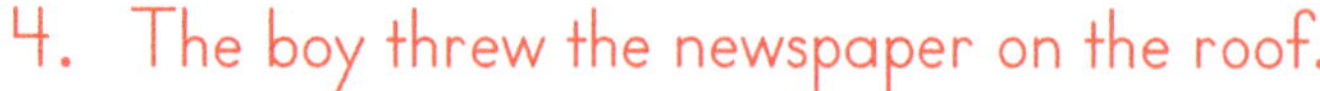
4. The boy threw the newspaper on the roof.

5. The toy canoe was Sue's souvenir.

Read the nouns. Write the plural form. Next, write sentences using each word.

1. baby ______________________

____

____

2. family ______________________

____

____

3. country ______________________

____

____

Read the words in bold print. Write a sentence that tells how the words are alike. Use the key word in the sentence.

1. **answer the telephone, use a computer, greet people**

   key word: secretary

   ____

   ____

2. **what to buy, where to go, when to go**

   key word: decisions

   ____

   ____

3. **basketball players, authors, movie stars**

   key word: autographs

   ____

   ____

4. **newspaper, dictionary, phone book**

   key word: information

   ____

   ____

5. **wigs, masks, hats**

   key word: costumes

   ____

   ____

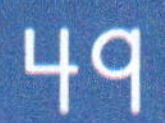

49

Read the sets of sentences. Rewrite them as one sentence.

Example:

I wore a costume.
It was a pirate costume.

I wore a pirate costume.

1. The caribou grazed in the meadow.
   It had large antlers.

____

2. I got a new bike. It is blue.

____

3. The zoo has a new tiger. It came from India.

____

4. I will go to the store. I will get peanut butter.

____

5. We rode in a canoe. It had a leak.

____

6. The cat climbed a tree. It was a tall tree.

____

Read the questions about the story, *Sole Winning*.
Answer them with complete sentences.

1. How did Matthew's Double Pump Slammer get lost?

2. Why did Buzz take Matthew's shoes?

3. What did Matthew think when he saw Buzz wearing his shoes?

4. What did Matthew learn in the story?

Read the descriptions. Match the number from the word list to the description.

1. astound	2. devour	3. boundary	4. encounter	5. fowl	6. chowder

_____ This can lay eggs.

_____ A hungry lion would do this to its prey.

_____ If you're hungry for soup, you might eat this.

_____ A surprise party might do this to you.

_____ This means to meet someone.

_____ This is the edge of something.

Read the words and definitions.

adventure: *something that is exciting and unusual*

attention: *the ability to listen, watch, or think carefully about something*

commotion: *to move in a loud way*

complain: *to say how you dislike things or speaking about having pain*

creature: *anything that is alive, especially animals*

daydream: *to imaging something (like a dream) while you're awake*

encourage: *to say or do things to make someone feel better*

introduce: *to bring in or identify*

refreshing: *to make cool or clean*

tremendous: *very large*

trustworthy: *dependable. Something or someone that will do what you think it should do.*

Read the words. Make new words with ou or ow by adding o, w, or u. Write the words on the lines.

1. non ____________________
2. muse ____________________
3. no ____________________
4. fund ____________________
5. don ____________________
6. so ____________________
7. shut ____________________
8. spot ____________________
9. clod ____________________
10. once ____________________

Read the sentences. Underline the verbs. Does the verb have the past, present, or future tense? Fill in the circle.

1. the goat climbed the mountain. ○ past ○ present ○ future
2. **The mouse is having a great adventure.** ○ past ○ present ○ future
3. I am eating this yummy brownie. ○ past ○ present ○ future
4. The cowboy is taking a shower. ○ past ○ present ○ future
5. The mayor will make the announcement. ○ past ○ present ○ future
6. The lady watered the flowers. ○ past ○ present ○ future
7. The chef used flour to bake cake. ○ past ○ present ○ future
8. Having success will encourage you. ○ past ○ present ○ future
9. He will complain about the cloudy skies. ○ past ○ present ○ future
10. The downpour was refreshing. ○ past ○ present ○ future

53

Read the analogies. Fill in the circle next to the word that completes them.

1. Girl is to woman as boy is to ____. ○ child ○ man ○ girl
2. Peel is to banana as fur is to ____. ○ coat ○ fruit ○ dog
3. Night is to day as tall is to ____. ○ short ○ high ○ big
4. Shovel is to dig as spoon is to ____. ○ knife ○ dirt ○ eat
5. Car is to tires as people are to ____. ○ drive ○ shoes ○ round
6. Sleep is to nap as jog is to ____. ○ run ○ jump ○ kick
7. Happy is to sad as ugly is to ____. ○ pretty ○ duckling ○ angry

Read the sentences. Write the missing word. Use words from your vocabulary list. The gray words are not used in the sentences. Create sentences for the three gray words on another piece of paper.

Vocabulary List: adventure, attention, commotion, complain, creature, daydream, encourage, introduced, refreshing, tremendous, trustworthy

1. The cool iced tea was very ____________.
2. The ____________ing child did not pay ____________ to the teacher.
3. The falling pans caused quite a ____________.
4. Did the boy ____________ about a headache?
5. What kind of ____________ has a long bushy tail?
6. Did the award ____________ you?
7. The man ____________ the boy to the girl.

Read the questions about the story, *Tidbit and the Bell*.
Answer them with complete sentences.

1. What did Mr. Blacky want to do to Tidbit?

2. How did Tidbit get to the rat's cage?

3. What did Fritz want to do with the bells?

Read the words and their figurative meanings.
Choose three and write sentences using figures of speech.

1. angel: kind, well-behaved
2. pig or hog: selfish
3. bear: grouchy or difficult
4. wolf: tricky and harmful

5. chicken: afraid
6. snake: sneaky and mean
7. doll: cute person
8. rock: faithful

56

Read the sentences. Underline the word that has the vowel digraph ea.
Fill in the circle that tells whether the ea makes a long e or short e sound.

1. I daydreamed that I was a monkey. O short O long
2. We ate toast for breakfast. O short O long
3. The snowy weather made it hard to travel. O short O long
4. Is summer your favorite season? O short O long
5. The threads on the baseball glove broke. O short O long
6. The leader was lost. O short O long

Read the sentences. The words in bold print are homophones.
Choose the correct homophone to complete the definitions.

The clerk **led** me to the batteries. The batteries have **lead** in them.

Can you **meet** me at the grocery store? We need to buy **meat** for the barbecue.

The workers picked **pears** from the trees. They filled a **pair** of baskets.

The **brakes** on the bicycle stopped working. That caused me to **break** the fence.

1. led	2. lead	3. meet	4. meat	5. pears	6. pair	7. brakes	8. break

_____ two of something

_____ are a kind of fruit

_____ to have been in front of the line

_____ is a kind of metal

_____ to join someone

_____ comes from animals

_____ to tear something up

_____ help you stop

Read the words. Write questions that the words will answer.

1. ears ______________________________
____
2. leaves ______________________________
____
3. break ______________________________
____
4. heart ______________________________
____
5. heaven ______________________________
____

Read the sentences. Look at the underlined word. How is it used in the sentence? Is it a noun or a verb? Fill in the correct circle.

1. He could not **bear** the hot weather. O noun O verb
2. The doctor will **treat** the wound. O noun O verb
3. We will use the heavy **thread** on the button. O noun O verb
4. The pheasant had brown feathers on its **head**. O noun O verb
5. The **treasure** sunk to the bottom of the sea. O noun O verb
6. The cleaver **bear** found the honey tree. O noun O verb
7. Grapes are a healthy **treat**! O noun O verb
8. Would you please **thread** the needle? O noun O verb
9. Always **treasure** the people you love. O noun O verb
10. In a fire, calmly **head** to the nearest exit. O noun O verb

58

Read the paragraphs. Write the sentences to answer the questions.

I hit the baseball as hard as I could. It sailed into the outfield. Arnold raced to the wall and almost caught it. The ball flew over the fence. It was a grand slam home run. I smiled all the way home.

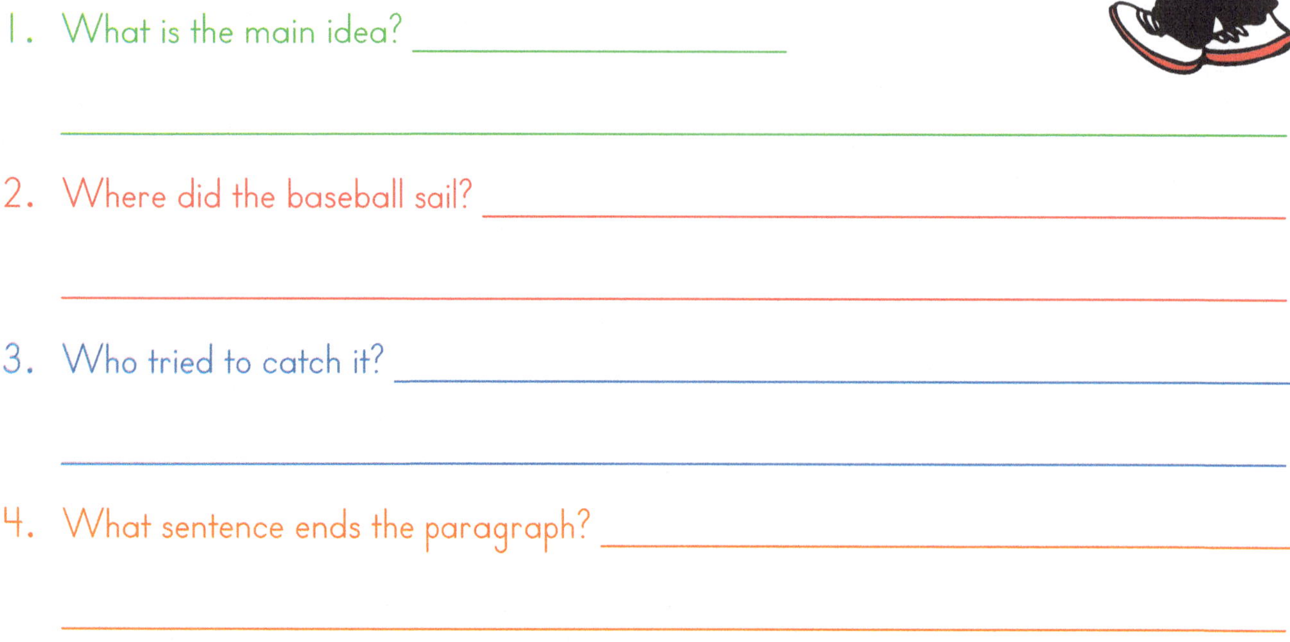

1. What is the main idea? ______________________

____

2. Where did the baseball sail? ______________________

____

3. Who tried to catch it? ______________________

____

4. What sentence ends the paragraph? ______________________

____

Fall is a very nice season. The leaves on the tree turn red. orange, and yellow. The weather is cool and pleasant. We feast on the fall harvest. These are just a few reasons for loving the autumn season.

5. What is the main idea? ______________________

____

6. What makes the fall nice? ______________________

____

7. What sentence ends the paragraph? ______________________

____

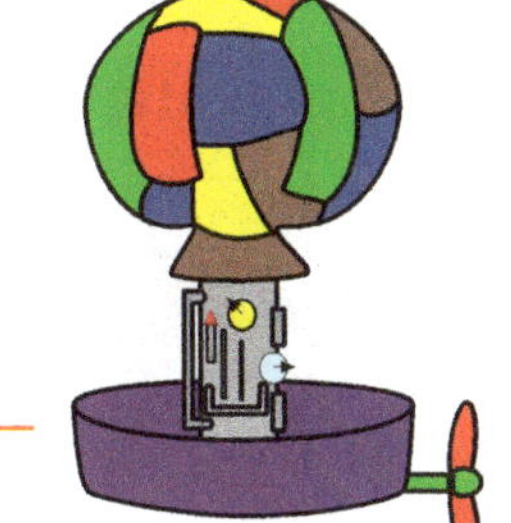

Read the questions about the story, *Tidbit to the Rescue*. Answer them with complete sentences.

1. How did Tidbit save Fritz from the snake? ______________________________

2. Why did Fritz think Tidbit's father had been captured? ______________________________

3. How did the basket catch fire? ______________________________

Read the groups of words. Write a sentence telling how the words are alike.

1. steak, peach, gingerbread
____

2. summer, autumn, winter, spring
____

3. snow, rain, sunshine
____

4. sea, pond, lake, ocean
____

5. leaves, roots, branches, trunk
____

61

The prefix pre often means before.

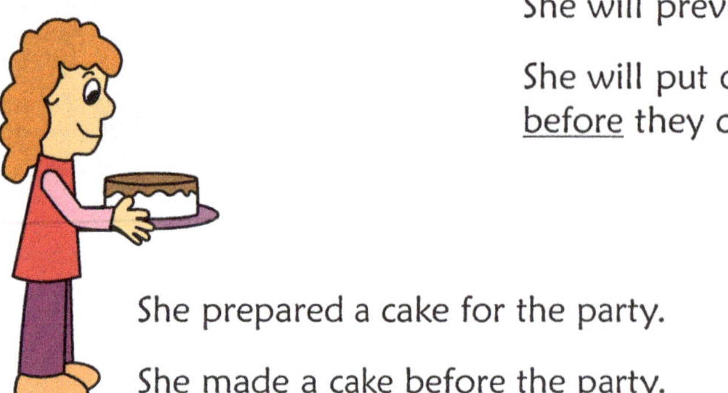

She will prevent a forest fire.

She will put out the flames before they cause a forest fire.

She prepared a cake for the party.

She made a cake before the party.

Sometimes you can find the meaning of the word if you know the meaning of the prefix and the root word.

Match the words and complete the definitions using root words. Choose a word from this list to fill in the box: **pretest, preschool, prepay, precaution, preexist, prejudge, precancel, prepackage**.

Write the root word to fill in the blank to complete the definition.

Example: precancel : to cancel a postage stamp before mailing.

1. ______ : To put something in a ______ before selling it.
2. ______ : To take a ______ before being taught something.
3. ______ : To ______ for something before you get it.
4. ______ : To use ______ before something bad happens.
5. ______ : To ______ before something else.
6. ______ : A ______ children attend before the age of 6.
7. ______ : To ______ before learning facts.

Proper names of people, places, and things are capitalized.

Places: St. Louis, Missouri, Oak Street, United States of America

People: Dr. Jones, Mr. Smith, King Leroy

Things: Chevy, McRuffy Press, Wal-Mart

Gateway Arch photo public domain National Park Service

Underline the letters that need to be capitalized.

1. Does roy live on boyd road?
2. Is boise the capital of idaho?
3. Did joyce buy the new toyota?
4. Has troy ever been to oakland, california?
5. Did you see joan in des moines, iowa?

Read the sentences. Underline the subject parts.

Example:

The tiny blue rowboat was filled with oysters.

1. Our new sleeping bags were moisture proof.
2. The blue sailboat left on a dangerous voyage.
3. The king employed servants to show hospitality.
4. The rough and tough cowboy liked sirloin steaks.
5. The yellow toaster oven cooked the tiny pizzas.

63

Read the whole paragraph with the missing words before choosing the correct answers. Choose words in the parenthesis for your answer. Circle the best answer.

The snake ____ (slithered, hid, coiled) through the brush. The little mouse was ____ (aware, afraid, unaware) of the danger it was in. It calmly nibbled on some ____ (snakes, seeds, eating) outside its cozy den. Just then the mouse heard the flutter of ____ (the snake, leaves, wings). A ____ (chicken, hawk, falcon) had swooped down onto the snake. The mouse ____ (watched, was caught, ate cheese) as the hawk flew away with a snake clutched in its talons. The hunter had become the prey.

Fill in the blanks using the vocabulary words in the box below.

confident	dangerous	hospitality	instructed	suspected	innocent

1. Mountain climbing is a ________________________ spot.

2. The guide ________________________ us on how to climb safely.

3. The girl showed great ________________________ to Tidbit.

4. The little girl was blamed, but she was ________________________.

5. Mr. Mouse was ________________________ that they were safe.

Read the questions about the story, *Fritz and the Fire*. Answer them with complete sentences.

1. Why did Tidbit like the new cage? ______

______

2. What happened to the owl when it came home? ______

______

3. What really caught the house on fire? ______

______

Read the sentences. Add details and change the sentences to answer the questions. Write the changed sentences.

1. The truck stopped. *Why did it stop?*

______

2. The frog croaked. *Where did it croak?*

______

3. The beagle ran. *Who owns the beagle?*

______

4. The teacher ate breakfast. *What did the teacher eat for breakfast?*

______

5. The bird caught the earthworm. *When did the bird catch the earthworm?*

______

Read the sentences. They describe a category. Write three words that fit each category.

1. People in a family

   1. ______________ 2. ______________ 3. ______________

2. Things you see in the sky

   1. ______________ 2. ______________ 3. ______________

3. Different kinds of pies

   1. ______________ 2. ______________ 3. ______________

4. Things you find in a field

   1. ______________ 2. ______________ 3. ______________

5. Foods that are fried

   1. ______________ 2. ______________ 3. ______________

Vocabulary: Read about stenotype.

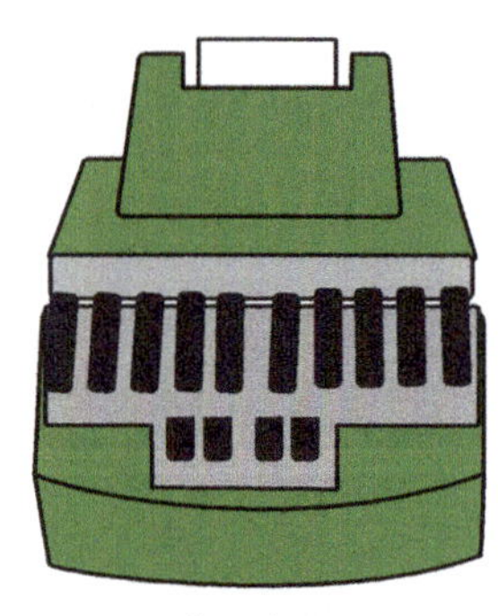

stenotype

1	2	3	4		6	7	8	9	
S	T	P	H	*	F	P	L	T	D
	K	W	R		R	B	G	S	Z

5	0		
A	O	E	U

Letters on the stenotype keyboard

Stenotype

It's important to keep a written record of what is said in a trial. Sometimes what is said needs to be repeated to make sure everyone understood what was said. It also helps ensure that the trial was fair to everyone. Someone who writes what is said is called a **stenographer**.

A stenographer uses a special keyboard to type words in a court trial. It's called a **stenotype**. People speak fast, so a stenographer has to type fast to keep up. They must type 200 to 300 words a minute.

Stenographers shorten words and sometimes spell words the way they sound instead of using correct spelling. Look at the letters. The keyboard doesn't even have all the letters, but stenographers use their own code for words. For example, cat might be spelled kat because there is no c on the keyboard. Later they type words the correct way.

Read the clues. Find the word from the word list that answers the clue or completes the sentence. Write the answers in the boxes.

Word List	
many	happy
fly	fifty
sly	friendly
grizzly	dragonfly
sloppy	angry
drizzly	pies
families	fry
slushy	shy
sleepy	lies
stories	my
dried	cry
everything	puppies

Across

1. The wet clothes needed to be ____.
3. Nice
5. ____ Bear – a kind bear
6. More than one family
9. Drowsy
10. Dog babies
12. forty, ____, sixty
13. The way birds move
14. A sad person does this
15. Belongs to me
16. Cherries or apples baked in a crust
18. Melting snow is ____.
19. Bashful
20. Mad

Down

1. A kind of bug
2. Rainy – a light, cold rain
4. A dishonest person does this
7. Opposite of sad
8. Messy
9. Books tell these
11. Opposite of nothing
13. A way to cook food
15. Opposite of few
17. Tricky, like a fox

Write a sentence telling what each simile means.

1. Trish felt like a fish out of water.

2. We'll be there as quick as a wink.

3. The truck was as slow as a turtle.

4. My throat is as dry as the desert.

5. The boy swims like a duck.

Read the questions about the story, *Bobcat Cowboys on Trial*. Answer them with complete sentences.

1. Who fell on Davey Beaver's tail?

2. Why did the sheriff take over the bailiff's job?

3. Why was Frazzle O'Hare so afraid?

4. What happened to the rat?

5. Why didn't the bobcats go to the courthouse?

Read the short story and answer the questions. You will need to make inferences to answer the questions.

This is one of my favorite days of the summer. Another box came in the mail just for me. The box was from my grandparents. Inside was a present. Mom was baking a special cake. It smelled just like hot cocoa. The frosting mom made reminded me of snow. Lots of my friends are going to be here soon. I think I know what one gift is. I hard it barking in the garage.

1. Why were friends coming to this person's house?

2. Were his or her grandparents going to be there?

3. What color was the icing on the cake?

4. What flavor was the cake?

5. What gift was in the garage?

Read the analogies. Fill in the circle next to the word that completes them.

1. Whale is to tiny as goldfish is to ____. ○ small ○ swim ○ girl

2. Food is to eat as car is to ____. ○ drive ○ gas ○ share

3. Blue is to color as square is to ____. ○ shape ○ green ○ circle

4. Minute is to second as foot is to ____. ○ mile ○ inch ○ hour

5. Happy is to frown as sad is to ____. ○ cry ○ snarl ○ smile

6. Talk is to telephone as writing is to ____. ○ letter ○ call ○ read

7. Sun is to yellow as grass is to ____. ○ graze ○ green ○ grape

8. Egg is to chicken as seed is to ____. ○ feather ○ tree ○ leaves

Write the missing part of the sentence.
Write an S in the box if you wrote the subject part.
Write a P in the box if you wrote the predicate part.

Example: [P] The huge fish *weighed forty pounds*.

1. [ ] ______________________ whispered to her brother.

2. [ ] The apple orchard ______________________.

3. [ ] The leather wallet ______________________.

4. [ ] ______________________ ate a sandwich on Thanksgiving.

5. [ ] ______________________ enjoyed the bright sunshine.

6. [ ] The new theatre ______________________.

7. [ ] ______________________ sat on the leather sofa.

8. [ ] The frightened opossum ______________________.

Answer the questions about *Bobcat Cowboys on Trial (part 2)*. Answer with complete sentences.

1. Why did the Bobcat Cowboys get in trouble at school?

2. Why did Frazzle O'Hare think the bobcats were kitty cats?

3. Why didn't the other animals see Billybob cheat at checkers?

4. Who was Peppy Possum?

5. Why did Bobbybill take too much pizza?

Read about the animals. Answer the questions on th next page.

Bobcats

Bobcats are a member of the cat family. They are called bobcats because they have short tails. Bobcats have spotted and striped fur coats. The fur is gray, tan or brown. The fur on their bellies is white. They have large paws and sharp claws.

A female bobcat will have a litter of two to four kittens. They may weigh four to eight ounces. Bobcats grow up to weigh twenty to thirty pounds. They are about thirty inches long.

Bobcats are good hunters. Their favorite food is rabbits or hares. They also eat other small rodents and birds. Sometimes bobcats will hunt larger animals such as deer and lambs. Most adult bobcats hunt and live by themselves.

Wolves

Wolves are related to dogs. They have long bushy tails. Wolves have thick fur. The color of the fur may be gray, white, or reddish. They have large paws with fur between their toes.

A female wolf will have a litter of four to seven pups. They grow to weigh between sixty and one hundred twenty pounds. Gray wolves are about eighty inches long. Red wolves are smaller.

Wolves hunt in packs. A pack is a group of wolves that live together. They hunt large animals such as deer, moose, and antelope. They also eat small rodents, birds, insects, and even berries.

Answer the questions about bobcats and wolves. Fill in the circle that tells what animal is being described. Fill in the circle for both if the questions describes both animals.

1. Which animals live alone? ○ bobcats ○ wolves ○ both

2. Which animals hunt deer? ○ bobcats ○ wolves ○ both

3. Which animals have spots? ○ bobcats ○ wolves ○ both

4. Which animals are a part of the dog family? ○ bobcats ○ wolves ○ both

5. Which animals can have four babies? ○ bobcats ○ wolves ○ both

6. Which animals can weigh over 100 pounds? ○ bobcats ○ wolves ○ both

7. Which animals have short tails? ○ bobcats ○ wolves ○ both

8. Which animals eat small rodents? ○ bobcats ○ wolves ○ both

9. Which animals live in packs? ○ bobcats ○ wolves ○ both

10. Which animals could have white fur? ○ bobcats ○ wolves ○ both

Answer the questions using the vocabulary words.

allergic	business	concerned	handsome	mathematical	theater
imaginary	creature	explain	dangerous	porcupine	serious

1. What kind of animal has quills? ____________
2. What is another word for animal? ____________
3. What is place to see a movie or a play? ____________
4. What kind of problem has numbers? ____________
5. What is a place people work? ____________
6. What is an opposite of funny? ____________
7. What means something that is not real? ____________
8. What means to tell how to do something? ____________
9. What is an opposite of ugly? ____________
10. What means worried or caring deeply? ____________
11. What means unsafe? ____________
12. What means to have an allergy? ____________

Add a prefix to each word to answer the question. Add pre, re, or un.

1. _______historic: before history was written
2. _______package: to package again
3. _______friendly: not friendly
4. _______fund: to give money back to someone who paid for something
5. _______tie: to take a knot out of something
6. _______heat: to warm up before cooking
7. _______grateful: not grateful
8. _______count: to count again
9. _______caution: being careful before something bad happens
10. _______write: to write something over

77

Some words can be both nouns and verbs. Read the sentences. A word is in bold print. Fill in the circle to tell if the word was used as a noun or a verb.

1. What **time** does the play start? ○ noun ○ verb
2. Can you **time** the race? ○ noun ○ verb
3. The full moon **lights** the sky. ○ noun ○ verb
4. The scared boy turned on the **lights**. ○ noun ○ verb
5. We can take a lunch **break** at noon. ○ noun ○ verb
6. Did the camera **break** when it hit the floor? ○ noun ○ verb
7. A roll of **tape** is in the drawer. ○ noun ○ verb
8. I can **tape** the torn dollar bill. ○ noun ○ verb
9. Did the children **catch** colds? ○ noun ○ verb
10. The outfielder made a great **catch**. ○ noun ○ verb

Read the sentences. Find the verbs. What is the tense of the verbs? Fill in the correct circles.

1. The beaver made a dam out of sticks. ○ past ○ present ○ future
2. The opossum will cook a pizza. ○ past ○ present ○ future
3. We are trimming the shrub. ○ past ○ present ○ future
4. The sunshine brightened the day. ○ past ○ present ○ future
5. The skydivers will use the new parachutes. ○ past ○ present ○ future
6. Thanksgiving dinner was very good. ○ past ○ present ○ future
7. The class is making leather belts. ○ past ○ present ○ future
8. Apples are growing in the orchard. ○ past ○ present ○ future
9. I wrote a paragraph about Christmas. ○ past ○ present ○ future
10. The girls will eat sandwiches for lunch. ○ past ○ present ○ future

Read each group of words. Find the statement that describes how the words are alike. Write the letter in the blanks.

_____	1. pizza, tires, pennies	A.	Kinds of small animals
_____	2. windshield, mirror, light bulb	B.	Three meal times
_____	3. butterflies, airplanes, chickens	C.	Things that are round
_____	4. breakfast, lunch, supper	D.	Things that have corners
_____	5. United States, Canada, Mexico	E.	Ways to describe how something looks
_____	6. nephew, uncle, grandfather	F.	Things that are made of glass
_____	7. rectangle, triangle, pentagon	G.	Things people are allergic to
_____	8. porcupine, opossum, groundhog	H.	Things that have wings
_____	9. dust, flowers, foods	I.	Kinds of relatives
_____	10. handsome, cute, beautiful	J.	Names of countries

Read the sentences. Fill in the circle next to the word that best completes the analogy.

1. Mountain is to climb as lake is to _____.	O small	O swim	O land
2. Nephew is to uncle as niece is to _____.	O other	O cousin	O aunt
3. Bobcat is to cat as wolf is to _____.	O dog	O muskrat	O cowboy
4. Eyebrow is to face as fingernail is to _____.	O nose	O foot	O hand
5. Rejoice is to happy as mourn is to _____.	O sad	O glad	O sleep
6. Continue is to stop as approach is to _____.	O go	O avoid	O run
7. Porcupine is to prickly as rabbit is to _____.	O soft	O quills	O carrot
8. Safe is to dangerous as hot is to _____.	O warm	O cold	O burn
9. Monster is to imaginary as moose is to _____.	O fake	O antlers	O real
10. Unwrap is to wrap as refill is to _____.	O prepare	O unfill	O fill

79

Read the story and answer the questions.

This was a terrible day to move. The big truck was late. We couldn't load things. We ran out of tape. Not all the boxes were sealed. Sheets of plastic covered the furniture. We didn't want it to get wet when it was carried outside. I'm glad we don't move often.

1. What is the main idea of the paragraph?

____

____

2. Why weren't all the boxes sealed?

____

____

3. Was the sun shining or was it rainy? ____________________ How do you know that?

____

____

4. Why weren't they loading things on the truck?

____

____

Use vocabulary words to complete the sentences.
Underline the other vocabulary words used in the sentences.

allergic	business	concerned	handsome	mathematical	theater
imaginary	creature	explain	dangerous	porcupine	serious

1. The ______________________________ is a creature with quills.
2. We saw a play at the ______________________________ about an imaginary rabbit.
3. You need to solve ______________________ problems to have a successful business.
4. We were very ______________________________ about the dangerous roads.
5. Being allergic to pets can be a __________________________ problem for a vet.

What two words were not used? ____

____

Choose words from the list to complete the sentences.

rough	bought	caught	beautiful	dough	through	sleigh

1. We ______________________ a pizza for ten dollars.
2. The sandpaper felt ______________________.
3. The baker placed the ______________________ in the oven.
4. Are you ______________________ with your homework?
5. The ______________________ glided across the snow.
6. The roses looked ______________________.
7. The baseball player ______________________ the fly ball.

Make a graphic organizer for *The Three Little Pigs.*

The Underground Railroad

In the early part of our country's history, not all people were free. People were captured in Africa. They were then taken aboard ships. The ships sailed to America

The African people became slaves in America. They weren't free to work or live where they chose. In fact, other people owned them. People who owned slaves were called masters.

The slave masters were sometimes very cruel to the slaves. They made the slaves work. They did not pay them. If a slave did not want to work, he was beaten with a whip. Sometimes the legs and arms of slaves were chained together.

If the master needed money, he could sell slaves to another master. Sometimes a mother or father was sold. Sometimes the children were sold. If that happened, they often times never saw each other again.

Many people thought this was very wrong. They tried to make slavery illegal. They also helped slaves escape from their masters. If someone was caught helping a slave escape, they could be put in jail. They might also have to pay a lot of money for fines.

Slave Auction

Still, there were many people willing to help slaves run away. The slaves ran away for lots of reasons. Some had cruel masters who hurt them. Others didn't want to be separated from other members of their families. Many slaves just wanted to be free.

The people helping slaves worked together. One day a slave was running away from his master. The slave jumped into a river. He began swimming. His master hopped in a boat. He watched the slave reach the other shore.

Soon, the master paddled to the place where the slave had landed. The slave master couldn't find the slave anywhere. The slave seemed to have just disappeared. He said the slave must have found an underground railroad.

There really wasn't a train that ran underground. The slave probably found some people to help him. So, the people who helped slaves escape started calling themselves workers on the "Underground Railroad."

Some states in those days allowed people to own slaves. Other states did not. These were called "free states." The slaves tried to run away to those states that didn't allow slavery. Most of these states were in the northern part of the United States. Many slaves ran away to Canada.

The slave owners paid lots of money to buy slaves. They were very upset when slaves ran away. They would chase them with dogs. Many times, slave owners offered large rewards for the return of their runaway slaves.

The slave owners also had laws passed. One law was passed in 1850. It was called The Fugitive Slave Act. A fugitive is someone who runs away.

It was a very bad law for all black people. Not all black people were slaves. Some were free. Most of the free black people lived in the free states.

The new law said the slave owners could take their runaway slaves from the free states. All they had to do was say a black person was their slave. The law didn't give the black person any rights. Even if they were really free, they could be made slaves if a slave owner lied.

Every free black person carried papers. The papers explained that they were free. But even that didn't stop some evil slave masters or slave hunters. They could simply take the papers away. Some free black people were kidnapped. They were then sold as slaves.

In 1863 President Abraham Lincoln set all the slaves free. Still, a war had to be fought. The Civil War ended slavery for good. That also ended the Underground Railroad. It was no longer needed.

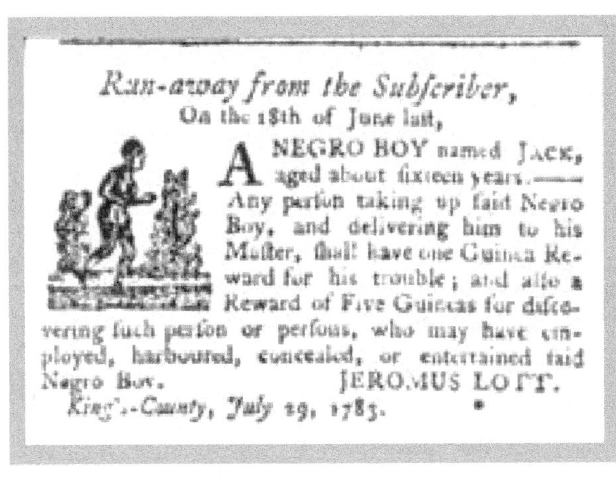

Run-away from the Subscriber,
On the 18th of June last,

A NEGRO BOY named JACK, aged about sixteen years.—— Any person taking up said Negro Boy, and delivering him to his Master, shall have one Guinea Reward for his trouble; and also a Reward of Five Guineas for discovering such person or persons, who may have employed, harboured, concealed, or entertained said Negro Boy.

JEROMUS LOTT.

King's-County, July 29, 1783.

Ad for a runaway slave boy

Read the sentences.
Write the predicate adjective on the first line.
Write the noun it describes on the second line.

Example: The bug is tiny.
Predicate Adjective *tiny* Noun *bug*

1. The old cow is brown.

   Predicate Adjective ______________ Noun ______________

2. The big hairy gorillas are funny.

   Predicate Adjective ______________ Noun ______________

3. My math book is thick.

   Predicate Adjective ______________ Noun ______________

4. The tennis shoes are old.

   Predicate Adjective ______________ Noun ______________

5. The new car is fast.

   Predicate Adjective ______________ Noun ______________

Read the sentences. Find the adjective and the adverb in each sentence. Words in the sentences are numbered. Write the numbers for the adjective and the adverbs.

1. The chocolate(1) doughnuts(2) quickly(3) disappeared(4).

_____ adjective _____ adverb

2. The youngest(1) daughter(2) laughed(3) loudly(4).

_____ adjective _____ adverb

3. We quickly(1) caught(2) up to the runaway(3) chimp(4).

_____ adjective _____ adverb

4. Throughout the storm a mighty(1) wind(2) violently(3) shook(4) the house(5).

_____ adjective _____ adverb

Read the sentences. Add at least one adjective and one adverb to each sentence and write the new sentence on the line.

1. The bus stopped.

____

2. The girl yelled.

____

3. The duck swam.

____

4. A bird chirped.

____

Negro Spirituals were songs that had a religious theme, but they also had hidden meanings. Slaves used the songs to communicate secret messages. They were often sung right in front of their masters. The masters just thought the slaves were singing about their faith. Harriet Tubman, an ex-slave, often used these songs on her trips into the south for the underground railroad. She would sing messages that could be passed along from one group of slaves to another.

Run to Jesus

I thought I heard them say,
There were lions on the way.
I don't expect to stay
Much longer here.

Run to Jesus - face the danger -
I don't expect to stay
Much longer here.

This song was used by a slave to let other slaves know they were planning to escape. What lines let you know the secret meaning?

____

____

____

Steal Away

Chorus: Steal away, steal away!
Steal away to Jesus!
Steal away, steal away home!
I ain't got long to stay here!

My Lord calls me!
He calls me by the thunder!
The trumpet sounds it ina my soul!
I ain't got long to stay here!

My Lord, he calls me!
He calls me by the lightning!
The trumpet sounds it ina my soul!
I ain't got long to stay here!

This song was used to call a meeting to talk about plans to revolt or run away. What lines do you think send this message?

____

____

____

Swing Low, Sweet Chariot

Swing low, sweet chariot,
Coming for to carry me home,
Swing low, sweet chariot,
Coming for to carry me home.

I looked over Jordan and what did I see
Coming for to carry me home,
A band of angels coming after me,
Coming for to carry me home.

If you get there before I do,
Coming for to carry me home,
Tell all my friends that I'm coming, too,
Coming for to carry me home.

This song was used to let slaves know that there was a wagon or other transportation in the area that could take them to the north and freedom. What lines do you think send this message?

____

____

____

Answer the questions about the story *Elijah's Coming*.
Write your answers on the lines.
Use complete sentences.

1. What was the job of the man that Elijah saved?

2. Who was the second person that came to Elijah's house?

3. What did Elijah hide in the hay?

4. What did the man discover was wrong with him when he woke up?

5. Why did Lizzy stop Elijah from getting the man some water?

Read the sentences. One of the words in each sentence is missing the prefix *over* or *under*. Write the correct prefix to complete the words in the sentences.

Over

Under

1. A helicopter flew ____________________head.
2. My library book is ____________________due.
3. The squishy apples are ____________________ripe.
4. Earthworms live ____________________ground.
5. The fat pig was ____________________weight.
6. Did you ____________________stand the directions?
7. Fish are ____________________water animals.
8. The puppy was ____________________joyed to see her master.
9. The ____________________cover policeman wore a disguise.
10. The boy was late because he ____________________slept.

Match the vocabulary word to the descriptions.

accident	curious	disguise	miracle	protection

1. We ______________________________ a pizza for ten dollars.
2. The sandpaper felt ______________________________.
3. The baker placed the ______________________________ in the oven.
4. Are you ______________________________ with your homework?
5. The ______________________________ glided across the snow.

Read the paragraph. Words are missing. One of the words in parentheses will work. Circle the correct word. Read the whole paragraph before making your choices.

Our family loves to ____. (camp, sing, play) We just bought a new ____. (car, boat, tent) Dad ____ me how to put together the poles. (taught, made, had) My brothers drove ____ into the ground. (earthworms, stakes, trucks) Mom ____ the poles through some loops. (sewed, pushed, lost) We all need to ____ together when we put our tent. (fight, play, work)

What part of speech matches the color of the words?
Fill in the circles to mark your answer.

We quietly watched the funny bear cubs.

- O noun O pronoun O verb O adverb O adjective
- O noun O pronoun O verb O adverb O adjective
- O noun O pronoun O verb O adverb O adjective
- O noun O pronoun O verb O adverb O adjective
- O noun O pronoun O verb O adverb O adjective

The young badger carefully sniffed the air in search of its next meal.

- O noun O pronoun O verb O adverb O adjective
- O noun O pronoun O verb O adverb O adjective
- O noun O pronoun O verb O adverb O adjective
- O noun O pronoun O verb O adverb O adjective
- O noun O pronoun O verb O adverb O adjective

Complete the analogies.

wife	car	sun	time	water

1. South is to direction as noon is to ______________________.
2. Bunny is to scary as ______________________ is to cold.
3. Boyfriend is to girlfriend as husband is to ______________________.
4. Earthworm is to dirt as fish is to ______________________.
5. Porch is to house as bumper is to ______________________.

Complete the sentences using vocabulary words.

accident	curious	disguise	miracle	protection

1. The ______________________ kitten climbed into the red box.
2. You should wear kneepads and a helmet for ______________________ while skateboarding.
3. The damaged car had been in an ______________________.
4. It was a ______________________ that nobody was hurt.
5. The long, gray beard is a part of my ______________________.

Answer the questions about the story *Elijah's Coming*.
Write your answers on the lines.
Use complete sentences.

1. What did Elijah find on the bridge?

2. Who saw Elijah's parents?

3. Why were Elijah's parents taken to the town?

4. What happened to Uncle Jermain and Mr. Shepard?

5. What do you think will happen next?

Read about the five food groups. Make an outline for the paragraphs.

There are five major groups of food. The first group is made up of meats, poultry, fish, dry beans, peas, eggs, and nuts. Hot dogs, chicken, and tuna fish belong in this group. The next group is dairy products. This includes milk, cheese, and yogurt.

Grains make up the next group. This would include bread, pasta, cereal, and rice. Another group is fruits. Bananas, oranges, and grapes are a part of this group. The last food group is the vegetable group. This includes carrots, potatoes, spinach, and broccoli.

Many other foods fit in these groups. Can you think of others?

I. Meats, Poultry, Fish, Dry Beans, Peas, Eggs, and Nuts
  A. Hot dogs
  B. ______________________
  C. ______________________

II. Dairy
  A. ______________________
  B. ______________________
  C. ______________________

III. ______________________
  A. Bread
  B. ______________________
  C. ______________________

IV. Fruits
  A. ______________________
  B. ______________________
  C. ______________________

V. ______________________
  A. ______________________
  B. ______________________
  C. ______________________
  D. ______________________

Read the sentences. A word is missing.
Fill in the circle next to the word that correctly completes the sentence.

Remember the definitions:

their: *belongs to them*
there: *a place*
they're: *a contraction for the words they are*

1. The books are over _____. ○ their ○ there ○ they're
2. _____ very good books. ○ Their ○ there ○ they're
3. _____ covers have great pictures. ○ Their ○ there ○ they're
4. _____ doing an experiment. ○ Their ○ there ○ they're
5. _____ parents watched them. ○ Their ○ there ○ they're
6. We will go _____ to see the results. ○ their ○ there ○ they're
7. I sat in _____ new car. ○ their ○ there ○ they're
8. _____ going to drive it to the library. ○ Their ○ there ○ they're
9. They will get a dictionary _____. ○ their ○ there ○ they're
10. Next, we will go to _____ house. ○ their ○ there ○ they're

Proper nouns should be capitalized. This includes the names of people, places, and things. Things can include books, movies, months, brand names, etc. Read the sentences. Circle the proper nouns that need to be capitalized.

1. She really enjoyed the movie cinderella.
2. Have you read the story little red ridinghood?
3. My birthday is in march.
4. The ford model-T was a very popular car.
5. The apollo 13 mission sent men to the moon.
6. Have you ever seen a movie starring john wayne?
7. The President lives in the white house.

92

Prepositions are words that link nouns or pronouns to other words in a sentence. When we describe the position of something, we tell where it is. Many prepositions are the key words in a sentence that tell where the noun is or where it is going.

Examples of prepositions:

above
to
by
out

○ behind	○ pretty	○ over	○ against	○ angry
○ quickly	○ under	○ bear	○ beside	○ across
○ the	○ in	○ carry	○ father	○ small
○ around	○ tall	○ on	○ below	○ near
○ out	○ ran	○ into	○ toward	○ underneath

Read the sentences. Circle the prepositions.

1. The sheriff was inside the jailhouse.
2. The library is behind the grocery store.
3. The puppy ran around the tree.
4. The raspberry bush was beside the cherry tree.
5. I stood between my parents.
6. The arrow sailed above the target.
7. You'll find lots of information in a dictionary.
8. I was embarrassed when I fell down.
9. Some bugs make their homes underneath rocks.
10. The grizzly bears ran across the meadow.

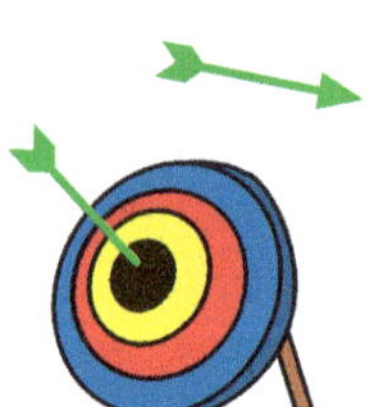

Read the story. Students will use the details of the story to answer the questions.

The Bobcat Cowboys robbed the First National Piggy Bank yesterday. They stole over three dollars worth of pennies. They were planning on using the pennies to buy gumballs from a machine.

Sheriff Prairie Dog chased the bank robbers all the way to Beary Bear's cave. The Bobcat Cowboys were hiding there to get away from the sheriff. They didn't know Beary was in the cave. The bear chased them all the way to the Rowdent Gulch jail.

1. Who robbed the bank? ______________________________
2. What did they steal? ______________________________
3. Where did they hide? ______________________________
4. When did they rob the bank? ______________________________
5. Why did they hide? ______________________________

____

Complete the sentences using vocabulary words.

biscuits	decision	identify	instructions	plantation

1. Could the sheriff ______________________ the bank robbers?
2. The slaves lived on a ______________________.
3. The ______________________ were made with flour.
4. The judge made a ______________________.
5. Did you follow the ______________________?

Answer the questions about the story *Elijah's Coming*.
Write your answers on the lines.
Use complete sentences.

1. Where did Mr. Jonas say he got the poster?

2. What was stuck to the newspaper?

3. What did the Judge do to Mr. Jonas?

4. How much money did the judge make Mr. Jonas pay Elijah's father?

5. What did Mr. Shepard trade for Lizzy?

Look at the pairs of words.
Write a sentence telling how the words go together.

1. Squid, squirrel ______________________________

____

2. Squeak, squeal ______________________________

____

3. Splash, stream ______________________________

____

4. Strawberry, throat ______________________________

____

5. Thread, string ______________________________

____

6. Spray, squirt ______________________________

____

7. Strike, throw ______________________________

____

Read the vocabulary list for *Matthew and Goliath*.

compassion	distraction	inexpensive
murmur	nervous	opportunity
persecute		

97

Complete the rhymes with words that begin with one of the three-letter blends.

sch	scr	shr	spl	spr	squ	str	thr

1. Would you get there sooner on a ship called a ______________________?
2. As long as they're free, I think I'll take ______________________.
3. The cat is hard to catch.
   It has sharp claws that ______________________.
4. If you need to tie a big thing, you'll need a lot of ______________________.
5. It's best not to quarrel with the fuzzy little ______________________?

Circle the possessive pronouns. Underline the words that show what the pronoun possesses.

1. The school bus screeched to a stop in front of her house.
2. My father used a screwdriver to assemble their new stroller.
3. The stranger threw a bone to his dog.
4. Our pet parrot liked to squawk at cats.
5. Your strawberry ice cream is starting to melt.
6. Whose squeegee did you use to clean the windows?
7. That scroll is mine.
8. The giant squid hid in its cave.
9. The square box is yours.

Read the pairs of sentences. Combine them into one sentence.

1. The sun was bright. It made me squint.

2. We waded in the stream. It was very cold.

3. I grew a huge squash. It was yellow.

4. The hawk began to shriek. It was very loud.

5. The girl sprained her ankle. She put it in a splint.

Write the vocabulary word that matches the description.

compassion	distracting	inexpensive	murmur	nervous	opportunity	persecute

1. Something that doesn't cost very much is ______.
2. Soft talking by a lot of people is a ______.
3. To be mean to people is to ______ them.
4. To be caring to someone is to show ______.
5. Loud noises can be ______.
6. To have the chance to do something is an ______.
7. To be afraid something bad could happen is to be ______.

Answer the questions about the story, *Matthew and Goliath*. Write your answers on the lines. Use complete sentences.

1. What happened to Stacy Lane?

2. What did the students give Nathan during recess?

3. How did Nathan get a black eye?

Complete the sentences using at least one word that begins with a three-letter blend.

sch	scr	shr	spl	spr	squ	str	thr

1. Did you buy the ______________________?
2. The shirt ______________________ when it was washed.
3. The king sat on his ______________________.
4. Who ______________________ the tube of toothpaste?
5. The man with big muscles was very ______________________.

Read the pairs of words. Are they antonyms or synonyms? Fill in the correct circle.

1. Danger: Safety — O antonym O synonym
2. Stranger: Friend — O antonym O synonym
3. Stitch: Sew — O antonym O synonym
4. Fidgety: Still — O antonym O synonym
5. Scratch: Scrape — O antonym O synonym
6. Exchange: Keep — O antonym O synonym
7. Knowledge: Wisdom — O antonym O synonym
8. Pledge: Promise — O antonym O synonym
9. Catcher: Pitcher — O antonym O synonym
10. Tasty: Yummy — O antonym O synonym

Read the sentences. A word is in bold print. Fill in the circle next to the word that is a synonym to the word in bold print.

1. She smothered the **pancakes** with syrup. — O cupcakes O breakfast O flapjacks
2. We played in the sand at the **seashore**. — O overseas O seacoast O season
3. The **snowstorm** lasted through the night. — O rainstorm O blizzard O snowshoe
4. All her money was in the **handbag**. — O purse O sack O handshake

Fill in the circle next to the word that is an antonym to the word in bold print.

1. The **cowboy** roped the steer. — O cowgirl O horseboy O bull
2. I looked **everywhere** for my books. — O everything O nowhere O wherever
3. Can we play baseball **outside**? — O outdoors O into O inside
4. **Grandpa** sent me that birthday card. — O grandson O grandma O grandfather

Read the vocabulary list for *Matthew and Goliath (part 2)*.

frustrated	choir	expressions
expected	attention	recognized
auditorium	assembly	

Read the sentences. Circle the articles. Underline the nouns that go with the articles.

Example:

1. The children played hopscotch.
2. We saw fish at a hatchery.
3. A smudge was on the windshield.
4. The watchdog growled at a stranger.
5. An angel was above the manger.
6. A sledgehammer is a heavy tool.
7. The partridge sat in a pear tree.
8. The fidgety boy had sat for over an hour.

Read the sentences. Fill in the word a or an.

1. The hedgehog ate ______ apple.
2. The farmer filled ______ manger with hay.
3. The stranger was ______ honest person.
4. ______ butcher chopped the meat.
5. ______ huge angel was in the painting.

Ranger's Pledge

There was a forest ranger
Who wasn't afraid of danger
He would often wrestle a bear
Just to sit in his office chair

One day a forest fire arose
He rushed to the flames with a hose
A badger helped to get control
But water flooded rabbit's hole

The ranger was both kind and brave
If he saw a need he always gave
When the rabbit began to cry
He said, "My home is warm and dry"

The ranger had too little knowledge
The rabbit's kids were home from college
So a cave is now the ranger station
Shared with a bear in hibernation

Writing to Instruct

Your latest "how-to" book, *Shoe Tying for Smarties*, was a great success!

Your publisher wants you to write a new "how-to" guide.

Choose what you want to teach. It's a short book (less than a page), so think of something simple. It can be a recipe, maybe explain how to do something in a sport, how to clean or fix something, or any other idea you might have.

Plan how you would tell someone how to do the activity. Expect that the readers of your book have little or no knowledge about the activity you're explaining. Think through all the steps. Maybe you can actually do the activity and think about each step you need to teach.

Explain the activity in your first draft. Use words like first, second, and next to help readers follow your steps in the process. You may also number your steps. It's important that your readers know when you begin a new step.

Test out your directions. Read them and try to do the activity using only your directions. Find and fix any mistakes that might make the directions unclear, including any spelling, punctuation, or grammar errors. Once all the errors are fixed, have someone else try your directions.

Edit anything that was difficult for others to follow. Make any corrections needed so that your directions are easy to follow. Add any needed steps or additional explanation. Eliminate steps or words that aren't needed and just make the directions more difficult to follow.

Illustrate steps that are difficult to describe. A picture can give a lot of information, but still use words to describe the steps.

Publish your directions and share your brilliance with the world!

Answer the questions about the story, *Matthew and Goliath*. Write your answers on the lines. Use complete sentences.

1. What happened to Matthew's lunchbox?

____

____

2. What animal scared the students in the assembly?

____

____

3. How did Mr. Day keep Nathan from getting hurt when the swing broke?

____

____

Read the paragraph. Answer the questions.

The ball bounced off the rim. Annie said ouch and rubbed her head. Cindy said she was sorry. The ball rolled away. Beth chased after it. Annie and Cindy yelled for her to stop. They didn't want Beth to get hit. Beth stopped just in time. The car honked as it passed by. Then she got the ball safely.

1. What hit Annie? ______________________________

2. Who threw the ball? ______________________________

3. Where did the ball roll? ______________________________

4. What almost hit Beth? ______________________________

5. What game were the girls playing? ______________________________

Read the words below. Write three compound words that contain the words in each list. You may use dictionaries.

rain	ball	some	down

Read the words. Which ones are compound words? Fill in the correct circles.

1. butterflies — O compound word — O not a compound word
2. tricycle — O compound word — O not a compound word
3. brainstorm — O compound word — O not a compound word
4. waterproof — O compound word — O not a compound word
5. decorate — O compound word — O not a compound word
6. knowledge — O compound word — O not a compound word
7. homemade — O compound word — O not a compound word
8. wagon — O compound word — O not a compound word
9. popcorn — O compound word — O not a compound word
10. compare — O compound word — O not a compound word

Read the sentences below. They contain some mixed-up compound words. Circle all the mixed-up words and write them correctly.

1. We are berryblue waffles for fastbreak. ______________________

____

2. The children found a great bookstory at the storebook. ______________________

____

3. The coachstage robbers had an groundunder outhide. ______________________

____

4. The noonafter shinesun dried up all the droprains. ______________________

____

5. The fishcat swam by the frogbull. ______________________

____

Read the words on the left. Fill in the circle next to the correct past tense form of the word. Circle the number before the word if it is an irregular verb.

1. break	O breaked	O broke
2. walk	O walked	O wolk
3. rent	O rented	O rant
4. freeze	O freezed	O froze
5. shrink	O shrinked	O shrank
6. swim	O swimmed	O swam
7. talk	O talked	O telk
8. write	O writed	O wrote
9. slip	O slipped	O slap
10. sit	O sitted	O sat

Read the sentences below. Put the correct ending mark on the blank. In the box, tell what kind of sentence the person spoke. Write Q if it is a question. S for statement. E for exclamation. C for command.

☐ 1. "Look out____" yelled the man.

☐ 2. The teacher said, "Line up at the door____"

☐ 3. "Did you see my keys____"

☐ 4. "Dolphins are mammals____"

Write a sentence that is a command and a sentence that is an exclamation below or on another paper.

____

____

____

____

Read the sentences. A word is in bold print. Fill in the circle next to the word that is a synonym of the word in bold print.

1. **Everyone** enjoyed the popcorn. ○ all ○ nobody ○ everywhere
2. The storm shelter is **underground.** ○ over ○ dirt ○ belowground
3. The plant needs lots of **sunlight.** ○ darkness ○ sunshine ○ moonlight
4. The **polecat** left a bad smell. ○ bobcat ○ skunk ○ hedgehog

Fill in the circle next to the word that is a antonym of the word in bold print.

1. We had pancakes for **breakfast.** ○ morning ○ mealtime ○ supper
2. **Something** is in those bushes. ○ nothing ○ someone ○ anything
3. Did you forget the **jellybeans**? ○ take ○ forgot ○ remember
4. The jail is **underneath** the courthouse. ○ basement ○ above ○ below

Complete the story using vocabulary words. One word will be used twice.

brainstorm	otherwise	meanwhile	tournament	expected	decorations

Otto was going to throw a party. It was for the winner of the big checker ____________________. He searched for his big box of ____________________. Otto searched and searched for the box. "Maybe I ought to sit down and ____________________ all the places it could be." Otto thought all afternoon. He couldn't remember what happened to the big box.

____________________, Bubba was the bigger winner. His brothers never ____________________ him to win. ____________________, they would have never stolen the box. Sheriff Prairie Dog arrested Billybob and Bobbybill. Bubba missed his brothers, so Otto threw the party in the jail.

"The jail looks very nice," said Bubba to his brothers.

"The ____________________ you stole makes the whole place look very festive."

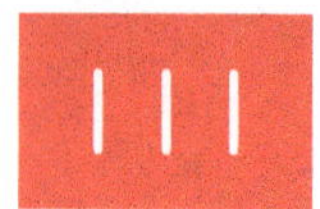

Read the definitions. Write a sentence using one of the words that begin with audi and write a sentence with a word that begins with auto.

The prefix **audi** means hearing or listening.

audible: *a sound that is loud enough to be heard*
audio: *the part you hear on television*
auditorium: *a large building for meetings or plays*

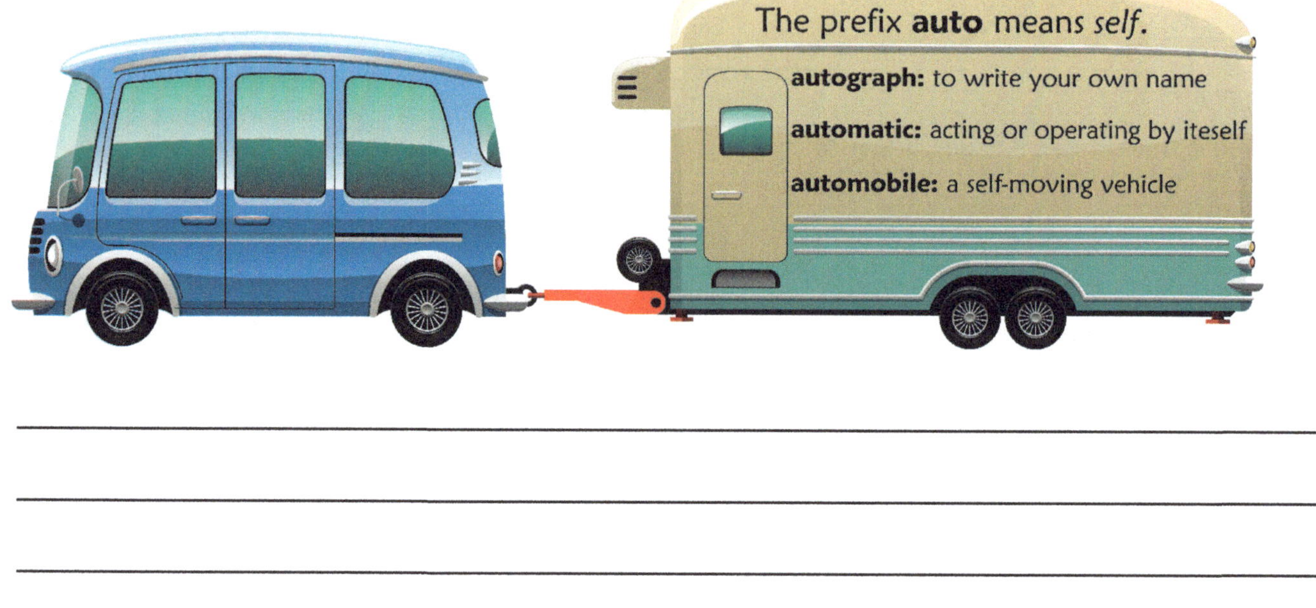

____

____

____

____

Read the definitions. Match the vocabulary words to the definitions. Write the words on the blanks.

annoyed	autograph	disguised	porridge	posse

1. Did you buy the ____________________.
2. The shirt ____________________ when it was washed.
3. The king sat on his ____________________.
4. Who ____________________ the tube of toothpaste?
5. The man with big muscles was very ____________________.

Read the sentences. The proper nouns need to be capitalized. Circle the proper nouns and write the capital letter above the beginning letters of the proper nouns.

S M B

Example: The dog named (skippy) ate a full box of (munchy bits.)

1. Did joe move to colorado in august?

2. tina is the youngest daughter of ted and elizabeth.

3. Is sydney a city in australia?

4. Will sam feed patch the parrot on tuesday?

5. The automobile sally drove was a jaguar.

6. We heard kelly sing in the largest auditorium in new york city.

7. The bobcat cowboys scared davey beaver.

8. Is alaska the biggest state in the united states?

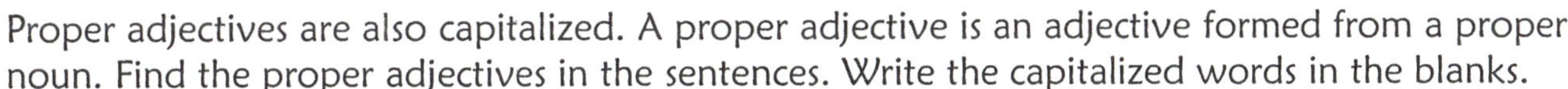

Proper adjectives are also capitalized. A proper adjective is an adjective formed from a proper noun. Find the proper adjectives in the sentences. Write the capitalized words in the blanks.

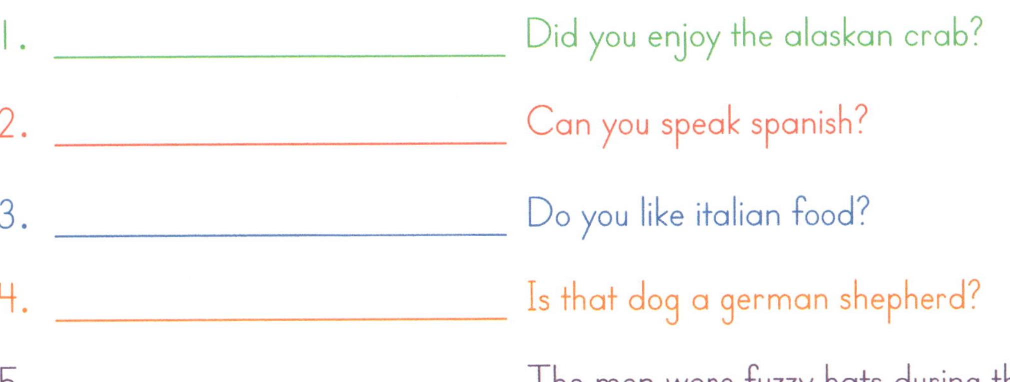

1. ____________________ Did you enjoy the alaskan crab?
2. ____________________ Can you speak spanish?
3. ____________________ Do you like italian food?
4. ____________________ Is that dog a german shepherd?
5. ____________________ The men wore fuzzy hats during the russian dance.

113

Label the boxes with one of the parts of speech that matches the words in the box. Pronouns, Nouns, Adjectives, Verbs, Adverbs, Articles. Add one word to each list.

pretty awful funny little sneaky	an the	crawled squawked coughed taught thought	saucer lawyer sausage audience daughter	loudly quickly slowly happily silently	his she we my your

What part of speech matches the color of the words? Fill in the circles to mark your answer.

Her spots helped the tiny fawn to easily blend into the brown leaves.

- O noun O pronoun O verb O adverb O adjective O article O preposition
- O noun O pronoun O verb O adverb O adjective O article O preposition
- O noun O pronoun O verb O adverb O adjective O article O preposition
- O noun O pronoun O verb O adverb O adjective O article O preposition
- O noun O pronoun O verb O adverb O adjective O article O preposition
- O noun O pronoun O verb O adverb O adjective O article O preposition
- O noun O pronoun O verb O adverb O adjective O article O preposition

The red-tailed hawk swiftly swooped down on its unsuspecting prey.

- O noun O pronoun O verb O adverb O adjective O article O preposition
- O noun O pronoun O verb O adverb O adjective O article O preposition
- O noun O pronoun O verb O adverb O adjective O article O preposition
- O noun O pronoun O verb O adverb O adjective O article O preposition
- O noun O pronoun O verb O adverb O adjective O article O preposition
- O noun O pronoun O verb O adverb O adjective O article O preposition
- O noun O pronoun O verb O adverb O adjective O article O preposition

Answer the questions about the story, The Bobcat Cowboys Steal the Show. Write complete sentences.

1. The bobcats were found guilty of what crime? ____________

2. Why did the Fowl Players steal the sleds? ____________

3. What business did Papa Prairie Dog and Davey Beaver start?

Read each sentence. Is it fact or opinion? Fill in the circle.

1.	Applesauce comes in a jar.	O fact	O opinion
2.	Australia is a beautiful continent.	O fact	O opinion
3.	That automobile is ugly.	O fact	O opinion
4.	The sausage tasted awful.	O fact	O opinion
5.	An author writes books.	O fact	O opinion
6.	That autograph is worthless.	O fact	O opinion
7.	The faucet is dripping.	O fact	O opinion
8.	August is the eighth month.	O fact	O opinion
9.	The auditorium had 500 seats.	O fact	O opinion
10.	The audience was very pleased.	O fact	O opinion

116

Write the missing letters to complete the words.

1. The old man c____________t a huge fish.
2. Our n____________bor is moving to a new town.
3. There is en____________ pizza for everyone.
4. The garden was filled with b____________tiful flowers.
5. I spent all afternoon str____________tening my room
6. The two cats started f____________ting over the milk.
7. Dad br____________t eighteen d____________nuts from the bakery.

Read the sentences. A word has been left out. Fill in the circle next to the missing word.

1. __________ standing by the roller coaster. O there O their O they're
2. The car is over __________. O there O their O they're
3. I have __________ phone number. O there O their O they're
4. __________ going to be so happy. O there O their O they're
5. __________ house is on the next street. O there O their O they're

Fill in the box at the beginning of each sentence to identify the type of sentence.
Write S for statement. Write Q for question. Write E for exclamation. Write C for command.

1. ☐ Are you going the auditorium?
2. ☐ That bike is so cool!
3. ☐ Take out your book and turn to page 176.
4. ☐ The little monkey was very curious.

Read the sentences. Answer the questions by making inferences.

1. Todd couldn't reach the books on the top shelf. Mark reached it for him.

   Who is taller, Todd or Mark? ______________________

2. Annie swung the bat. The ball sailed over the fence.

   What game was Annie playing? ______________________

3. We went to the store. I looked at puppies. My sister looked at the kittens. Dad liked the reptiles.

   What kind of store was the family visiting? ______________________

4. Megan rode the new sled down the hill. It was much faster than the old one.

   What covered the ground? ______________________

5. The nail started to bend. Fred kept pounding.

   What tool was Fred using? ______________________

Read the vocabulary words and definitions. Write numbers to match them.

______ a contest playing a sport or game

______ extremely tired

______ a large room with a stage

______ to believe something will happen

______ to make someone feel better

______ to identify something from a memory

______ a chance to do something

______ taking attention away from a task

______ to tell what something looks like

______ something that was not planned

1. Accident
2. Auditorium
3. Distracting
4. Encourage
5. Exhausted
6. Expect
7. Identify
8. Opportunity
9. Recognize
10. Tournament

Read the sentences. Circle the proper nouns. Underline the possessive pronouns. Write the articles in the box.

1. Thomas spilled his drink on the table.
2. Our friends caught a fish in Jordan Lake.
3. The map of the Atlantic Ocean is on your desk.
4. Julie found an orange spot on her new dress.
5. My dog Fluffy hurt its paw on the rocks.

Complete the analogies. Fill in the circle next to the best answer.

1. Feat is to feet as tail is to	O horse	O ears	O tale
2. Poodle is to dog as parrot is to	O bird	O partridge	O fly
3. Boat is to water as bus is to	O stop	O school	O street
4. Rock is to hard as pillow is to	O sleep	O soft	O bed
5. Book is to read as apple is to	O eat	O tree	O pie

Read the verbs. Write the past tense of each verb. Is it a regular or irregular verb? Fill in the circle.

1. break ____________ O regular O irregular
2. talk ____________ O regular O irregular
3. eat ____________ O regular O irregular
4. throw ____________ O regular O irregular
5. play ____________ O regular O irregular
6. see ____________ O regular O irregular
7. say ____________ O regular O irregular
8. cook ____________ O regular O irregular
9. know ____________ O regular O irregular
10. zip ____________ O regular O irregular

Fill in the blank with a vocabulary word.

1. A good education gives you a better ____________ to be successful.
2. My brother was ____________ me while I did my homework.
3. I am ____________ the package to arrive today.
4. The ambulance rushed to the ____________.
5. The boy did not ____________ the stray dog.
6. I was ____________ after the long race.
7. My uncle won the bowling ____________.
8. The audience left the ____________.
9. Can you ____________ the lost watch?
10. The girl was ____________ to play the piano.

accident
auditorium
distracting
encourage
exhausted
expect
identify
opportunity
recognize
tournament

121

Helping Verbs work with a main verb in the sentence.
The list contains the most common helping verbs.

Helping Verbs

am	being	did	has	might	was
are	been	do	have	must	were
be	can	does	is	shall	will
	could	had	may	should	would

To be a helping verb, the sentences must also contain a main verb to help. Some of these short words can also be used as linking verbs, linking the subject and predicate parts of sentences. Look at the two sentences below.

In the first sentence the word *are* is a linking verb. It links the two subjects (Tom and Mary) to the predicate (at the store).

In the second sentence, *are* is a helping verb. It helps the verb *shopping* and helps define the correct tense for the sentence.

are as a **linking verb**	Tom and Mary **are** at the store.
are as a **helping verb**	Tom and Mary **are** shopping at the store.

Read the sentences. Add the helping verbs and rewrite the sentences. Change the verb if necessary.

1. The horses pulled the carriage. Add the helping verb, **were.**

____

2. We drive to the beach. Add the helping verb, **might.**

____

3. The twins cleaned their room. Add the helping verb, **should.**

____

4. The guard arrested the thief. Add the helping verb, **had.**

____

5. The tailor fixed the queen's dress. Add the helping verb, **is.**

____

Match the descriptions to the words.

1. its	6. you're
2. your	7. too
3. there	8. their
4. two	9. to
5. they're	10. it's

_______ toward a place

_______ also, more, very

_______ a number

_______ the possessive form of it

_______ the contraction of it and is

_______ the possessive form of you

_______ the contraction of you and are

_______ the possessive form of them

_______ a place

_______ the contraction of they and are

Match the descriptions to the words.

1. The leopard was _____ years old. ○ to ○ too ○ two
2. _____ going to be very happy. ○ Their ○ There ○ They're
3. ___ almost time to leave. ○ Its ○ It's
4. The apple was _________ sour. ○ to ○ too ○ two
5. ________ someone very special. ○ Your ○ You're
6. Can we go _____ later? ○ their ○ there ○ they're
7. Do you have ________ tickets? ○ your ○ you're
8. _____ cookie recipe was the best. ○ Their ○ There ○ They're
9. The cobbler used thread ____ sew. ○ to ○ too ○ two
10. The hawk dropped _____ lunch. ○ its ○ it's

123

Complete the analogies. Fill in the circles next to the best answers.

1. Fish is to ocean as bear is to — O forest O teddy O grizzly
2. Trip is to tip as play is to — O swing O pray O pay
3. Board is to tree as French fry is to — O potato O ketchup O nails
4. Hour is to minute as mile is to — O smile O pint O feet
5. Bee is to honey as cow is to — O grass O moo O milk
6. Fork is to spoon as guitar is to — O piano O string O play
7. Pencil is to eraser as book is to — O read O page O mark
8. Am is to are as was is to — O where O were O wash
9. Friend is to enemy as build is to — O like O building O destroy
10. Cat is to leopard as dog is to — O coyote O puppy O bark

Read the sentences. Take out the helping verb and rewrite the sentences. Change the verb if necessary.

1. The snow had melted off the roof.

____

2. It could take an hour.

____

3. The dog did chase the cat.

____

4. The carriage had traveled ten miles.

____

5. The floodlight will turn off in the morning.

____

Read the descriptions. Write the vocabulary word to match each description.

carriage	cobbler	noblemen	tailor	guard

1. Someone who is rich and powerful. ___________________________
2. Someone who makes clothes. ___________________________
3. Someone who makes sure things are safe. ___________________________
4. Something a king would ride in. ___________________________
5. Someone who makes shoes. ___________________________

If you were a king or queen what laws would you make?
Write at least three laws. Use complete sentences.
You can write more on another piece of paper.
Your laws can be serious or silly and fun.
Include what happens if the law is broken.

____

____

____

____

____

____

____

____

Read the sentences. Write two more sentences that compare to the first sentence.
Add er and est to the adjectives.

1. The cricket is loud.

____

____

2. The math assignment is easy.

____

____

3. The ditch is deep.

____

____

4. The spaghetti is long.

____

____

Read the vocabulary words and definitions. Write the words next to the matching definitions.
Circle the two words that are synonyms.

restaurant	customer	café	constantly	impression

1. _______________ a place to buy food that has already been prepared
2. _______________ always, all the time, not stopping
3. _______________ someone who buys something
4. _______________ something that is remembered
5. _______________ a place to buy food that has already been prepared

Subject and Verb Agreement

Nouns and verbs that are related in sentences must have matching forms. If a noun is singular, the verb should be singular. If the noun is plural, the verb must be plural. Many **nouns** are made **plural** by adding an s at the end of them. Many **verbs** become **singular** when an s is added at the end.

singular The dolphin leaps from the pool.

plural The dolphins leap from the pool.

Read the sentences. Correct the sentences. Write the sentence with the noun corrected. Then, write the sentence with the verb corrected. Write the plural sentence on the first line and the singular sentence on the second line.

1. The wrapper cover the candy.

Plural ____________________

Singular ____________________

2. The yacht sail to the island.

Plural ____________________

Singular ____________________

3. The cake need an egg yolk.

Plural ____________________

Singular ____________________

4. My neighbor know a plumber.

Plural ____________________

Singular ____________________

Add the words more and most to the sentences to show sentences that compare things. Use different nouns. For example: Tom is handsome. Sam is more handsome. Bob is the most handsome.

1. The snake is frightening.

____

____

2. The wrench is useful.

____

____

What part of speech matches the color of the words?
Fill in the circles to mark your answer.

We carefully searched the cave on the rocky side of the island for a treasure chest.

O noun O pronoun O verb O adverb O adjective O article O preposition
O noun O pronoun O verb O adverb O adjective O article O preposition
O noun O pronoun O verb O adverb O adjective O article O preposition
O noun O pronoun O verb O adverb O adjective O article O preposition
O noun O pronoun O verb O adverb O adjective O article O preposition
O noun O pronoun O verb O adverb O adjective O article O preposition
O noun O pronoun O verb O adverb O adjective O article O preposition

Fill in vocabulary words to complete the sentences.

restaurant	customer	café	constantly	impression

1. Your politeness will make a good ______________________.
2. I ate a burger and fries at the ______________________.
3. The wind ______________________ blows down that sign.
4. The waitress works at the new ______________________.
5. That ______________________ purchased the last snow shovel.

Spelling Pre-test: Fill in the circles next to the correctly spelled words.

1.	O desine	O dessign	O design	O designe
2.	O plumber	O plumer	O plummer	O plumner
3.	O musile	O muscle	O muscel	O musle
4.	O waitless	O weightless	O wateless	O waytless
5.	O rhmey	O ryhme	O rhyme	O rimhe
6.	O handsome	O hanbsome	O handsum	O hanbsume
7.	O nuckle	O knuckle	O knukle	O knucal
8.	O spageti	O spagheti	O spaghetti	O spugetti
9.	O tung	O tungue	O tonge	O tongue
10.	O knowlege	O nauleje	O knowledge	O noledge
11.	O skecht	O scech	O scetch	O sketch
12.	O half	O haf	O haugh	O hafe
13.	O iren	O iron	O irn	O iryon
14.	O iland	O eyeland	O island	O ilanm
15.	O whraper	O whrapper	O hrapper	O wrapper

130

Read each list of three words. Write sentences to compare the words.

1. car, cheetah, rocket

2. candy, fruit, cake

Answer the questions about the story, Big Tom's Café.
Write complete sentences.

1. How did the cafe get its name?

2. Why did Buddy and Gracie run the restaurant by themselves?

2. What did they feed their customers?

Number Prefix Chart

bi	2
cent	100 or 1/100
dec	10
di	2
duo	2
hepta	7
hexa	6
kilo	1000
milli	1/1000
nona	9

oct	8
pent	5
poly	many
quint	5
quart	1/4 or 4
quad	4
sept	7
tri	3
uni	1

Read the questions. Use the chart to find the answers. Write the answers on the lines.

1. The root meaning for –cycle is circle. Wheels are circles.
   How many wheels do these have?

   bicycle ____ tricycle ____ unicycle ____

2. Different sized singing groups have different names based on the number of people in them. How many people are in each of these singing groups?

   quintet ____ quartet ____ septet ____ trio ____ duo ____

3. The root meaning for –pod or –ped is feet. How many arms or feet do these animals have?

   octopod ____ biped ____ hexapod ____ quadruped ____ tripod ____

4. The root meaning of the –let is small. Babies are small.
   How many babies were born at the same time?

   quadruplet ____ triplet ____ septuplets ____ quintuplet ____

5. The root meaning of –gon is angles. The number of angles in a shape is the same as the number of sides in a shape. How many sides do these shapes have?

   nonagon ____ decagon ____ heptagon ____ octagon ____

   pentagon ____ triangle ____ hexagon ____

Fill in vocabulary words to complete the sentences.

noun	pronoun	adjective	adverb	verb	article

The silly clown skillfully rode a tiny unicycle.

The ______________ silly ______________
clown ______________ skillfully ______________
rode ______________ a ______________
tiny ______________ unicycle ______________

A huge octopus quickly snatched the angry lobster.

A ______________ huge ______________ octopus ______________
quickly ______________ snatched ______________ the ______________
angry ______________ lobster ______________

The new binoculars helped us see clearly.

The ______________ new ______________ binoculars ______________
helped ______________ us ______________ see ______________
clearly ______________

Read the definitions. The teacher will ask you questions.

____ **Combination:** *two or more things added together*

____ **Dickering:** *to talk about making a trade or a deal*

____ **Inspector:** *an official who makes sure things are as they should be*

____ **Invested:** *to spend money to make a profit*

____ **Livestock:** *farm animals such as cows, horses, sheep, chickens, and pigs*

____ **Professional:** *having great skill, doing something to be paid*

Use the Number Prefix Chart to answer the questions.

bi	2
cent	100 or 1/100
dec	10
di	2
duo	2
hepta	7
hexa	6
kilo	1000
milli	1/1000
nona	9

oct	8
pent	5
poly	many
quint	5
quart	1/4 or 4
quad	4
sept	7
tri	3
uni	1

Fill in the number that answers each question.

1. How many years are in a century? ____________
2. If you cut a pie into quarters, how many pieces will you have? ____________
3. How many grams are in a kilogram? ____________
4. A tricuspid is a tooth with how many points? ____________
5. How many years are in a decade? ____________

Read the sentences. Add a linking verb.

1. The quarter ____________ silver.
2. The bug might ____________ a centipede.
3. The triplets ____________ very cute.
4. The stop sign ____________ red.
5. I ____________ thirsty.

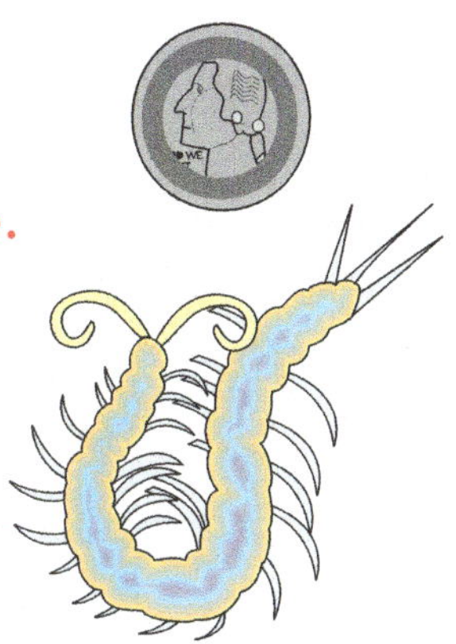

Linking Verbs
am are be being been is was were

Write a factual sentence and an opinion sentence about each word.

1. Octopus

Fact

Opinion

2. Tricycles

Fact

Opinion

3. Quarters

Fact

Opinion

Circle the words that should be capitalized.

1. Is the hawaiian monk seal and endangered animal?
2. The health inspector's name is mrs. gray.
3. Did uncle rocky give you the pigs?
4. Have you ever visited omaha nebraska?
5. Did you do well on the english test?
6. The new york yankees scored in the first inning
7. The scottish highland is a fuzzy cow.
8. The pigs names were abner and rex.
9. Have you ever visited rocky mountain national park?
10. The pigs ate breakfast at big tom's café.

Fill in the blanks with the correct vocabulary words.

1. The ______________________ said the building was in good shape.
2. I got the autograph of the ______________________ baseball player.
3. Purple is a ______________________ of blue and red.
4. My chores were to feed the ______________________.
5. The two men were ______________________ over the price of the horse.
6. Dad ______________________ a lot of money in the business.

135

Pigs in the Pancakes Graphic Organizer

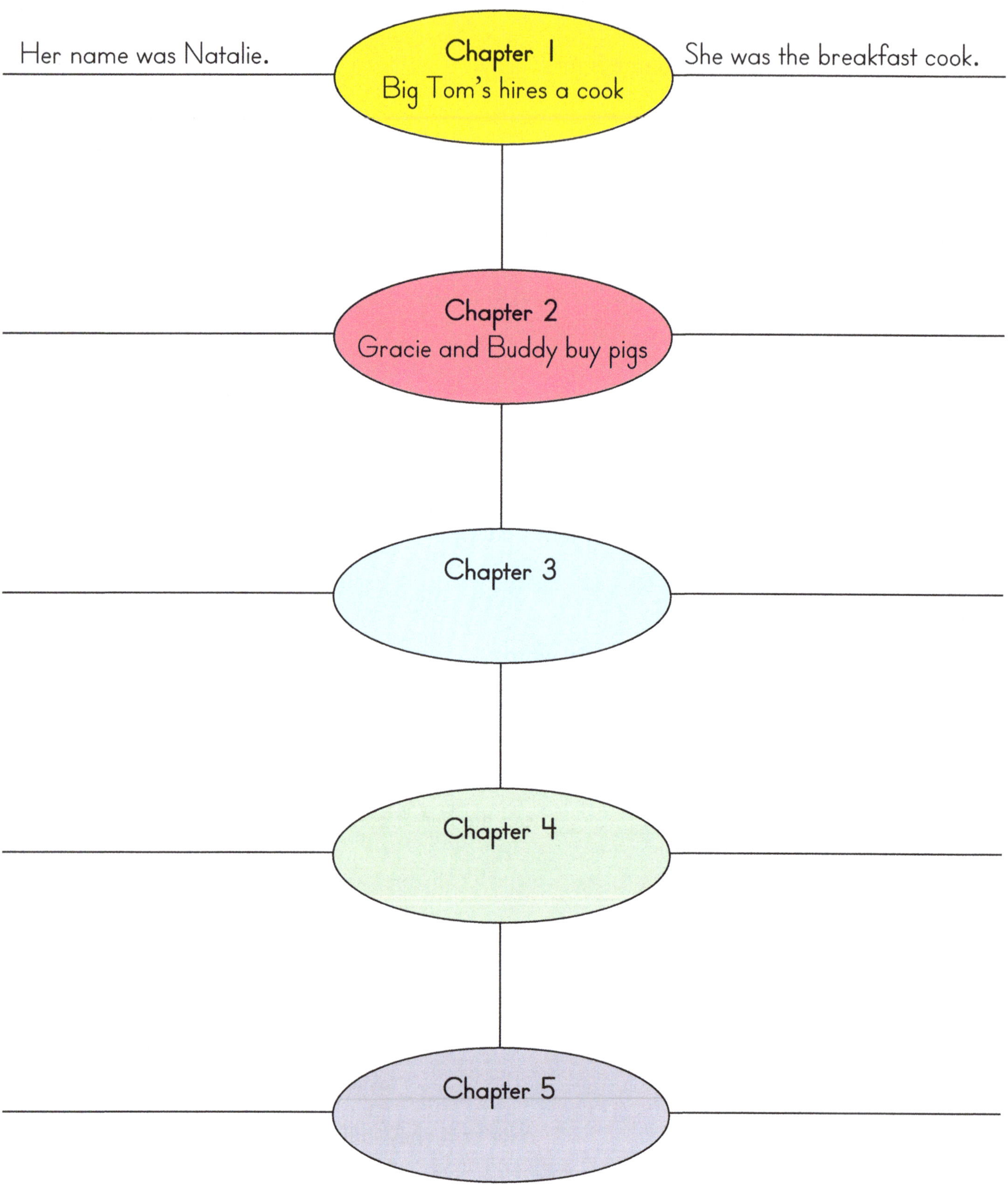

Read the sentences. Write the nouns from each part of the sentences.

1. The red octopus left its underwater cave.

Subject ____________________

Predicate ____________________

2. The hungry children ate the chocolate cake.

Subject ____________________ Predicate ____________________

3. The orange bicycle had a flat tire.

Subject ____________________ Predicate ____________________

4. The huge sponge soaked up the milk that was accidentally spilled.

Subject ____________________ Predicate ____________________

5. The kind ranger wore an official badge.

Subject ____________________ Predicate ____________________

Match the vocabulary words to the definitions. Write the words on the lines.

____________	*having to do with cats, including house cats, lions, tigers, and other members of the cat family*
____________	*an animal that eats other animals or their eggs*
____________	*keeping eggs warm until they hatch*
____________	*acting carefully in a dangerous situation*
____________	*a type of flower*
____________	*fierce*

cautiously
daffodil
feline
ferocious
incubation
predator

137

Read the statements.
Write two questions that can
be answered by the statement.

1. The circus opens tomorrow.

2. Nancy rode the bicycle.

3. That castle is in Germany.

4. We performed a dance in the pageant.

5. The giant log in the road caused the car accident.

Write the vocabulary words that complete the sentences.

cautiously	daffodil	feline	ferocious	incubation	predators

1. Tigers, bobcats, and cougars belong to the ____________________ family.
2. She placed the yellow ____________________ in a vase.
3. The roaring sounded ____________________.
4. A lot of ____________________ eat rabbits.
5. The chicks hatched after several days of ____________________.
6. We ____________________ crossed the street.

What part of speech matches the color of the words?
Fill in the circles to mark your answer.

The yellow flowers grew quickly beside the old house.

O noun O pronoun O verb O adverb O adjective O article O preposition
O noun O pronoun O verb O adverb O adjective O article O preposition
O noun O pronoun O verb O adverb O adjective O article O preposition
O noun O pronoun O verb O adverb O adjective O article O preposition
O noun O pronoun O verb O adverb O adjective O article O preposition
O noun O pronoun O verb O adverb O adjective O article O preposition

Did they find the geography and science books on top of the brown shelf?

O noun O pronoun O verb O adverb O adjective O article O preposition
O noun O pronoun O verb O adverb O adjective O article O preposition
O noun O pronoun O verb O adverb O adjective O article O preposition
O noun O pronoun O verb O adverb O adjective O article O preposition
O noun O pronoun O verb O adverb O adjective O article O preposition
O noun O pronoun O verb O adverb O adjective O article O preposition

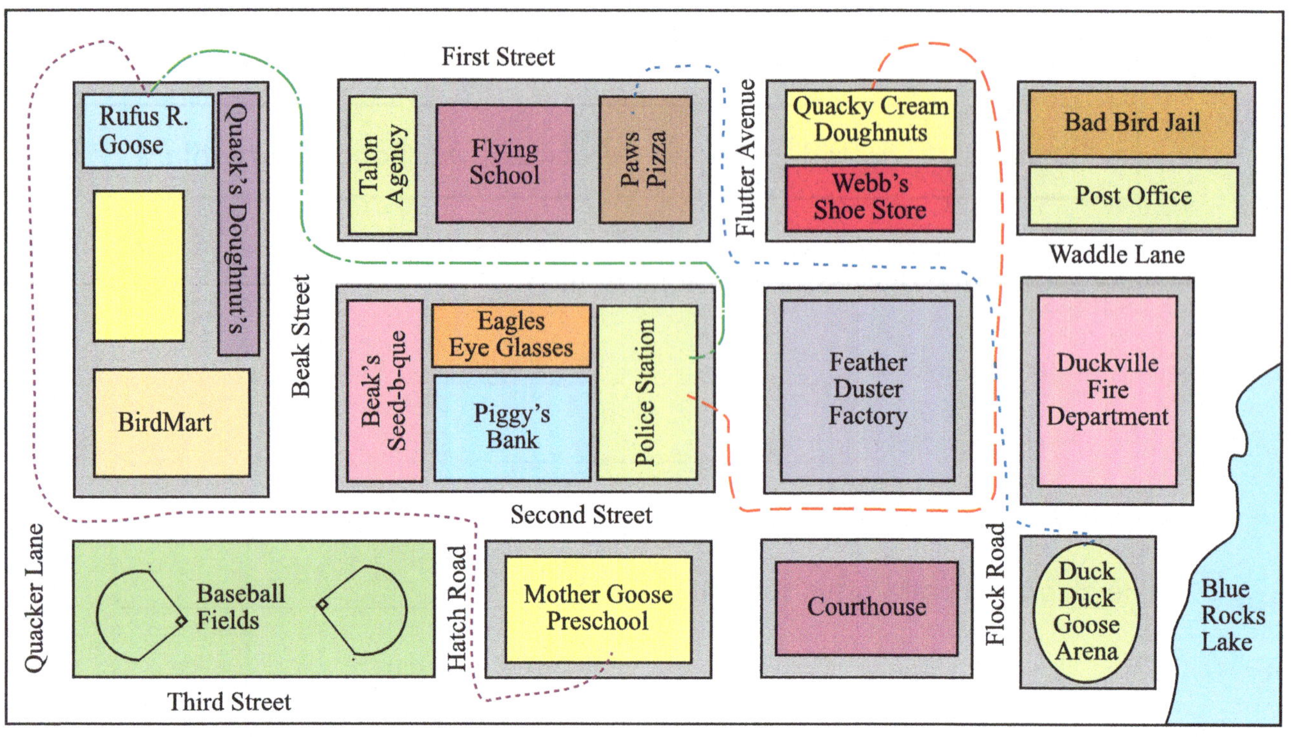

Look at the map. Write directions to answer the questions.

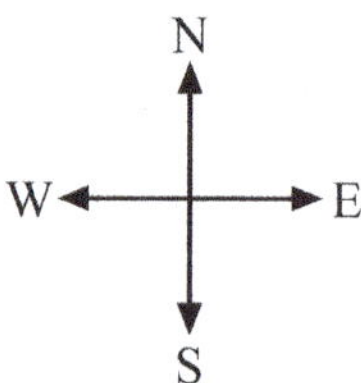

1. Rufus looked for eggs at Mother Goose Preschool. How did he get there? Follow the purple line.

2. Puffy and Rufus went to the Police Station. How did they get there? Follow the green line.

3. The police looked for Lightfingers Lenny at Quacky Cream Doughnuts. How did they get there? Follow the Red line.

Match the vocabulary words to the definitions.
Write the words on the lines.

undercover	delightful	distracting	cygnets

_______________ *young swans*

_______________ *describes something that brings great joy*

_______________ *something that is taking your attention away*

_______________ *doing something secretly or with a disguise*

Complete the analogies. Fill in the circles next to the best answers.

1.	Fire is to engine as base is to	O smoke	O ball	O first
2.	Minute is to time as mile is to	O distance	O inches	O hours
3.	Stack is to stackable as bend is to	O flexible	O bendable	O bending
4.	Enjoyable is to fun as squeezable is to	O laugh	O bounce	O soft
5.	Viewable is to invisible as adorable is to	O ugly	O adore	O lovable
6.	Sinkable is to wet as closeable is to	O closet	O shut	O clothes
7.	Curable is to cure as drivable is to	O boat	O walk	O drive
8.	Land is to farmable as people are to	O teachable	O children	O human
9.	Remarkable is to mark as removable is to	O movable	O remove	O move
10.	Cheese is to sliceable as boxes are to	O stackable	O printable	O winnable

Add a noun to either the subject part or the predicate part. Rewrite the sentence.

1. Peanut butter is good to eat on bread.

Peanut Butter

Add a noun to the subject ______________________________

____

____

2. Trisha plays soccer.

Add a noun to the predicate ______________________________

____

____

Add a noun to the subject ______________________________

____

____

grrr

3. The puppy growls at snakes.

Add a noun to the predicate ______________________________

____

____

Write a sentence that tells how the things in the lists are alike.
Choose a word from the key word list to use in the sentence.

sliceable	teachable	comfortable	enjoyable	disposable	portable

1. Dirty diapers, paper plates, dead batteries

2. A soft chair, your favorite clothes, a bed

3. Playing a game, going on vacation, a favorite dessert

4. A small radio, a cell phone, a tent

Write vocabulary words to match the descriptions.

undercover	delightful	distracting	cygnets

1. Watching television while doing school work ____________________
2. Something that hatched from an egg ____________________
3. Going on a picnic on a bright and sunny day ____________________
4. A police officer that is working in secret ____________________

Complete the analogies.

forgivable	profitable	questionable	bendable
portable	uncomfortable	sinkable	

1. Enjoyable is to pleasurable as movable is to ____________________
2. Code is to decodeable as give is to ____________________
3. Guessable is to unknowable as floatable is to ____________________
4. Unbelievable is to believable as unquestionable is to ____________________
5. Soft is to comfortable as hard is to ____________________
6. Fashion is to fashionable as profit is to ____________________
7. Fixable is to repairable as flexible is to ____________________

Read the paragraphs. Change it by using different words for the subjects.

1. Buster did not recognize Puffy Paws. Buster barked at Puffy Paws. Puffy Paws hissed at Buster. Puffy Paws was not afraid of Buster. Puffy Paws put on a lion disguise. Buster ran up a tree to get away from Puffy Paws.

Change some of the ways the subject was named in the paragraph to make the writing more interesting. Fill in the blanks.

Buster did not recognize Puffy Paws. ________________ barked at ________________. Puffy Paws hissed at ________________.

________________ was not afraid of Buster.

________________ put on a lion disguise.

________________ ran up a tree to get away from Puffy Paws.

2. Tony is nine years old. Tony's sister is Holly. Holly is seven years old. Holly and Tony like to go horseback riding. Tony and Holly feed cows. Tony and Holly live on a ranch.

Change some of the ways the subject was named in the paragraph to make the writing more interesting. Fill in the blanks.

Tony is nine years old. ________________ sister is Holly. ________________ is seven years old. Holly and Tony like to go horseback riding. ________________ feed cows. ________________ live on a ranch.

146

Read the paragraph. Answer the questions about cause and effect for numbers 1, 2, and 3. Follow the directions for numbers 4 and 5.

The pitcher threw the ball right down the middle of the plate. The batter swung. The ball sailed into the stands. My brother caught the ball. The crowd cheered for my brother.

1. What was the effect of throwing the ball down the middle of the plate?

____

2. What caused the crowd to cheer?

____

3. What caused the brother to catch the ball?

____

4. Write a cause for the effect: The bird flew away.

____

5. Write an effect for the cause: The rain poured down.

____

Match the vocabulary words to the definitions. Write the words on the lines.

		Word Bank
____________	*a set of straps that fit over an animal's head to allow it to be controlled*	corral
____________	*an area with a fence around it to keep animals from wondering away*	bridle
____________	*a small amount of food eaten before a meal*	mutton
____________	*famous for doing something wrong*	appetizer
____________	*meat from sheep*	notorious

Write the word that matches the description. Use words from the word list. Not all the words will be used.

delightful	bashful	thoughtful	needful	speechless	painful	worthless
shoeless	doubtful	sleepless	suspenseful	powerful	humorless	

1. causes pain ____________
2. barefoot ____________
3. really needed ____________
4. not sure ____________
5. not funny ____________
6. shy ____________
7. very strong ____________
8. full of delight ____________
9. unable to talk ____________
10. awake all night ____________

Read the sentences. Add adjectives to the noun in either the subject part or the predicate part. Add the adjective to the part listed before the sentence. Rewrite the sentence. Choose adjectives from the word list. Not all words are used.

harmless	rightful	helpless	beautiful	restless	cheerful
sleeveless	powerful	hairless	skillful	priceless	colorful

1. Predicate: The bobcat chased the duck.

____

2. Subject: The paint fell on my shirt.

____

3. Predicate: The bus was filled with children.

____

4. Subject: The dog was returned to its owner.

____

Read the sentences. Circle the prepositions.

1. The beautiful princess is inside the tower.
2. The seedless oranges are still on the tree.
3. The colorful pictures are above the fireplace.
4. The weightless astronaut floated over the spacecraft.
5. The worthless tires are beside the rusty cars.

Add a preposition to each sentence to correct it.
Write the sentences on the lines.

1. The bridle is hanging the post.

____

2. The colorful jacket fell the hanger.

____

Match the vocabulary words to the descriptions.

mutton	bridle	appetizer	notorious	corral

____________ *It's like a snack.*

____________ *Something a horse might wear*

____________ *This keeps farm animals in a small area*

____________ *Sheep would rather you not eat this.*

____________ *Famous outlaws are this.*

Combine each group of sentences into one sentence. Keep all the words that end with less or ful in the combined sentence. For example:

The toothache was painful. It left me joyless. I was sleepless because of it.

The painful toothache left me joyless and sleepless.

1. My brother, Thomas is bashful. He is also helpful. Thomas is cheerful.

____

____

2. The gum was delightful. It was also sugarless. After buying it, I was penniless.

____

____

3. The shoeless man sat on a corner. He was also toothless. It was thoughtful to help him.

____

____

Match the vocabulary words to the descriptions.

mutton	bridle	appetizer	notorious	corral

1. The ______________ outlaw robbed the train.
2. The spicy chicken wings were an ______________.
3. The cowboys drove the cattle into the ______________.
4. We put the ______________ on the horse.
5. The roast was ______________.

150

Read the paragraphs. Cross out the sentences that don't belong.

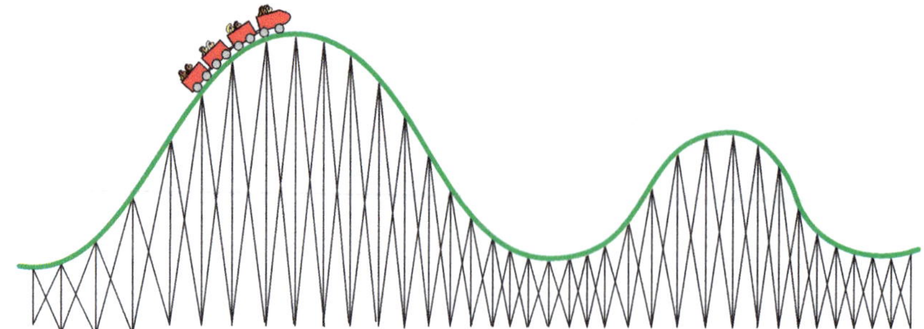

1. I was excited to ride the roller coaster for the first time. It was tall and fast. The first hill felt like I was falling into a bottomless pit. I wore my most colorful shirt. I was thankful the seatbelt held me in.

2. My sister plays softball. We played the first soccer game of the season today. It was a scoreless tie with seconds to go. Just as I got the ball, my shoe fell off. I had to make a shoeless kick. It was still a powerful kick. It was also painful. The ball soared past the goalie and we won the game.

3. It's important to be careful when hiking. Stay on the paths and don't wander off. Try to be watchful of harmful snakes and other animals. Enjoy the colorful flowers and butterflies. Follow the safety rules and hiking can be harmless and fun.

4. You have to be very skillful to fly a jet. A pilot can never be careless. You have to be watchful at all times for other aircraft. You can fly above the clouds. A good pilot should make a flight seem uneventful.

5. I found the puppy beside the road. It appeared to be motherless and fatherless. We put an ad in the paper, but the rightful owners never called. I'm grateful because I really liked the pup. My new pup can do tricks for doggie treats.

Find the root words. Take the suffixes and prefixes off the words.
You may need to add a letter to the root word.

1. capitalize ______________________
2. perfection ______________________
3. payment ______________________
4. education ______________________
5. mysterious ______________________
6. officer ______________________
7. unknowledgeable ______________________
8. neighborhood ______________________
9. measurement ______________________
10. unfriendly ______________________

Complete the similes. You may add more than one word.

1. The boy danced like ____.
2. I'm as hungry as ____.
3. The horse can run like ____.
4. My dad is as strong as ____.
5. It was as cold as ____.
6. She was as pretty as ____.
7. The shirt was wet like ____.
8. The perfume smelled like ____.

Write a simile of your own.

____

152

Complete the similes. You may add more than one word.

1. The happy muskrat gleefully gnawed on our dried cattails.

	The	happy	muskrat	gleefully	gnawed	on	our	dried	cattails.
noun	○	○	○	○	○	○	○	○	○
pronoun	○	○	○	○	○	○	○	○	○
adjective	○	○	○	○	○	○	○	○	○
verb	○	○	○	○	○	○	○	○	○
adverb	○	○	○	○	○	○	○	○	○
article	○	○	○	○	○	○	○	○	○
preposition	○	○	○	○	○	○	○	○	○

2. Their dangerous lion stalked angrily around the small cage.

	Their	dangerous	lion	stalked	angrily	around	the	small	cage.
noun	○	○	○	○	○	○	○	○	○
pronoun	○	○	○	○	○	○	○	○	○
adjective	○	○	○	○	○	○	○	○	○
verb	○	○	○	○	○	○	○	○	○
adverb	○	○	○	○	○	○	○	○	○
article	○	○	○	○	○	○	○	○	○
preposition	○	○	○	○	○	○	○	○	○

3. The sleepy children slowly walked up the steep stairs.

	The	sleepy	children	slowly	walked	up	the	steep	stairs.
noun	○	○	○	○	○	○	○	○	○
pronoun	○	○	○	○	○	○	○	○	○
adjective	○	○	○	○	○	○	○	○	○
verb	○	○	○	○	○	○	○	○	○
adverb	○	○	○	○	○	○	○	○	○
article	○	○	○	○	○	○	○	○	○
preposition	○	○	○	○	○	○	○	○	○

Complete the analogies using words from the list.

sad	sleep	freeze	harmful	sofa	happy	safe	room	sit	ice

1. Unfriendly is to friend as unhappily is to ______________________.
2. Darkness is to light as dangerous is to ______________________.
3. Cafeteria is to eat as hotel is to ______________________.
4. Equipment is to construction as furniture is to ______________________.
5. Hot is to evaporate as cold is to ______________________.

Match the definitions to the vocabulary words. Write the words on the lines.

concentrate	evidence	reception

______________________ *proof about a crime*

______________________ *to think about only one thing*

______________________ *a party after a big event like a wedding*

Write the vocabulary words that complete the sentences.

1. I had to really ______________________ to alphabetize the words.
2. The discovery of the ______________________ helped solve the crime.
3. The children ate lots of food at the ______________________.

Look at the picture of the moose in someone's front yard. Pretend you have to write a newspaper article based on this picture.

Use the 5 w's to help organize your story: who, what, where, when, and why.
Give your article a title on the top line.

Complete the graphic organizer by adding two details from each chapter.

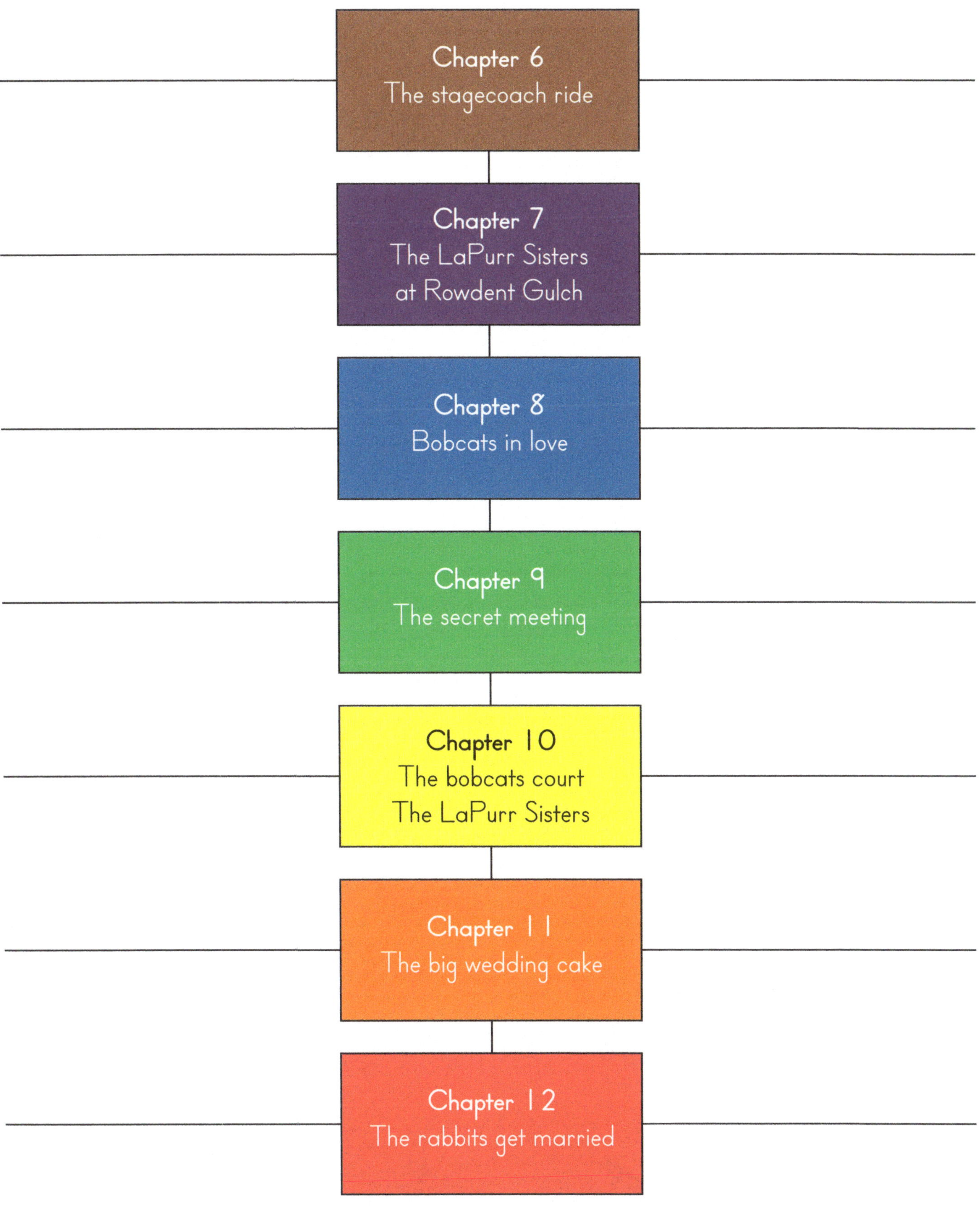

Complete the sentences using words from the list.

leopard	canoe	girl	islands	honest	tongue	listening	building	wrench	foreign

1. The state of Hawaii is several ______________________.
2. A ______________________ is a type of spotted cat.
3. My father works in that ______________________.
4. Her sister is a pretty ______________________.
5. I rode in a ______________________ down the river.
6. It's better to be ______________________ than to tell lies.
7. We loosened the bolt with a ______________________.
8. The hot chocolate burned my ______________________.
9. Have you ever visited ______________________ country?
10. Are you ______________________ to the radio?

Read the sentences. Add a helping verb from the list and rewrite the sentences.

Helping Verbs: am are can could did do does had has have is may might must shall should was were will would

1. I need two egg yolks for the recipe.

____

2. Judge Polecat send the coyote to jail

____

3. Our neighbors buying a yacht.

____

4. The badgers leave the forest.

____

Vocabulary Review List: Read the definitions. Write a sentence for each word.

Carriage (care-aje): *a fancy wagon pulled by horses*

____

Concentrate: *to think about only one thing*

____

Constantly: *always, all the time, not stopping*

____

Customer: *someone who buys something*

____

Cygnets: *newly hatched swans*

____

Delightful: *something that brings great joy*

____

Livestock: *farm animals such as cow, horses, sheep, chickens, and pigs*

____

Ferocious: *fierce*

____

Notorious: *famous for doing something wrong*

____

Predator: *an animal that eats other animals or their eggs*

____

157

Use the chart to answer the questions. Write the answers in the blanks.

bi	2	cent	100	dec	10	di	2
duo	2	hepta	7	hexa	6	kilo	1000
milli	1/1000	nona	9	oct	8	pent	5
poly	many	quint	5	quart	4	quad	4
sept	7	tri	3	uni	1		

1. If a mother had quintuplets, how many children did she have at one time? ______
2. If you heard a quartet sing, how many people did you hear sing? ______
3. If you drew a nonagon, how many sides would it have? ______
4. If your tooth is a bicuspid, how many points does it have? ______
5. If an animal is a hexapod, how many legs does it have? ______

Read the sentences. Are they facts or opinions? Fill in the correct circle.

1. The sidewalk is two miles long ○ fact ○ opinion
2. I have the best cookie recipe. ○ fact ○ opinion
3. A yacht is a type of boat. ○ fact ○ opinion
4. The gnats are very annoying. ○ fact ○ opinion
5. Ghost stories are frightening. ○ fact ○ opinion
6. My finger has a knuckle. ○ fact ○ opinion
7. Christmas is in December. ○ fact ○ opinion
8. This wrench works very well. ○ fact ○ opinion
9. This steak tastes great. ○ fact ○ opinion
10. The badger lives in the forest. ○ fact ○ opinion

Do the words have the hard or soft c or g sound? Fill in the circle for your answers.

1. carrot	O hard	O soft		2. century	O hard	O soft
3. official	O hard	O soft		4. acorn	O hard	O soft
5. discuss	O hard	O soft		6. dangerous	O hard	O soft
7. engine	O hard	O soft		8. again	O hard	O soft
9. gymnasium	O hard	O soft		10. cypress	O hard	O soft

Complete the analogies. Fill in the circles.

1. Bicycle is to two as tricycle is to — O ride O three O wheels
2. Gentleman is to lady as boy is to — O girl O man O woman
3. Orange is to fruit as lettuce is to — O green O eat O vegetable
4. Mouse is to mice as house is to — O hice O houses O home
5. December is to month as Tuesday is to — O day O May O year

Fill in the circle that correctly completes the sentences.

1. The calves ____________ in the pasture. — O run O runs
2. The ____________ use softened butter. — O recipe O recipes
3. The leopard ____________ the antelope. — O wrestle O wrestles
4. My ____________ are sore. — O knuckle O knuckles
5. The ____________ is on Main Street. — O building O buildings

Read the paragraphs and the statements. For each of the effects, write the cause.

The little spider went up the water spout. Down came the rain. It washed the spider out. Out came the sun. It dried up all the rain. The tiny spider went up the spout again.

1. What caused the spider to be washed out of the spout?

___

2. What caused the rain to dry up?

___

The big bad wolf huffed and puffed. The house of sticks fell down. The little pigs ran to the brick house. The little pigs got away. The wolf ordered a pizza, instead.

3. What caused the house of sticks to fall down?

___

4. What caused the wolf to order pizza?

___

The porridge was too hot to eat. The bears went for a walk. A little girl came to the bears' house. She sat at the table to eat porridge. The little chair broke. Baby Bear was sad when he came home from the walk.

5. What caused the bears to go for a walk?

___

6. What caused baby bear to be sad?

___

7. What caused the chair to break?

___

Read the words. Write the root words.

1. winnable ____________________
2. uneventful ____________________
3. measurement ____________________
4. enjoyable ____________________
5. unbelievable ____________________
6. precaution ____________________
7. asleep ____________________
8. knowledgeable ____________________
9. unselfish ____________________
10. frightening ____________________

Fill in the circle under each word that tells how the word is being used in the sentence.

1. The playful kitten quickly pounced on a plastic mouse.

	The	playful	kitten	quickly	pounced	on	a	plastic	mouse
noun	○	○	○	○	○	○	○	○	○
pronoun	○	○	○	○	○	○	○	○	○
adjective	○	○	○	○	○	○	○	○	○
verb	○	○	○	○	○	○	○	○	○
adverb	○	○	○	○	○	○	○	○	○
article	○	○	○	○	○	○	○	○	○
preposition	○	○	○	○	○	○	○	○	○

2. The colorful peacock strutted proudly around our new barnyard.

	The	colorful	peacock	strutted	proudly	around	our	new	barnyard
noun	○	○	○	○	○	○	○	○	○
pronoun	○	○	○	○	○	○	○	○	○
adjective	○	○	○	○	○	○	○	○	○
verb	○	○	○	○	○	○	○	○	○
adverb	○	○	○	○	○	○	○	○	○
article	○	○	○	○	○	○	○	○	○
preposition	○	○	○	○	○	○	○	○	○

Complete the sentences using vocabulary words.

1. The bank robber was a ______________________ thief.
2. The large, white horse pulled the beautiful ______________________.
3. The ______________________ followed the mother swan.
4. The ______________________ bought three bags of groceries.
5. The sunny day made the picnic ______________________.

Write the vocabulary word that matches the definition.

carriage	delightful
concentrate	ferocious
constantly	livestock
customer	notorious
cygnets	predator

1. ______________________ *farm animals*
2. ______________________ *very fierce, scary*
3. ______________________ *an animal that eats other animals*
4. ______________________ *the time*
5. ______________________ *to think about one thing*

Read the words. Circle the silent letters.

1. league
2. wrinkle
3. yolk
4. honest
5. knowledge